Nell

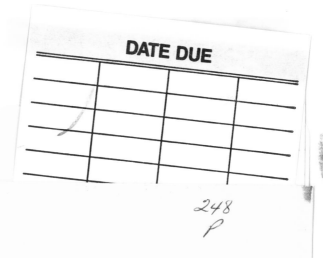

## DATE DUE

248
P

DEMCO

Chula Vista

# THE PROMISE
# OF PARADOX

# THE PROMISE OF PARADOX

## A celebration of contradictions in the Christian life

## Parker J Palmer

**Ave Maria Press** **Notre Dame, Indiana**

To Sally

# Contents

Introduction   11

## 1
In the Belly of a Paradox   15

## 2
The Stations of the Cross: A Meditation   45

## 3
Paradoxes of Community   59

## 4
A Place Called Community   67

## 5
A World of Scarcity—A Gospel of Abundance   93

## 6
The Conversion of Knowledge   111

# Introduction

It is a real joy for me to introduce this first book by Parker Palmer. It is the joy that grows from friendship. I met Parker for the first time only five years ago and today I can hardly think of my life and work apart from the crucial role that Parker has played in them. The many hours we have spent eating together, playing together, dreaming together, talking together, studying together, reading together, writing together, and most of all praying together, have laid the basis for a supportive, nurturing and creative friendship.

This friendship has allowed me to see the pages of this book being born from Parker's own direct struggles with life and its many options and possibilities. Parker has shown me how true it is that you don't think your way into a new kind of living but live your way into a new kind of thinking. Every part of this book is a reflection of a new kind of living in which Parker and his family have engaged. Parker's life story contains all the elements which contribute to making a well-known scholar: he studied theology, received a Ph.D. in sociology, taught at universities, did successful work as a community organizer, and wrote many remarkable articles. But this book is not the direct fruit of all of these accomplishments. On the contrary, it is the fruit of the many questions with which Parker bracketed these accomplishments. It is born out of the courageous and often agonizing critique of his own social, educational and religious development. This book is indeed the beautiful fruit of contradictions which became paradoxes: the contradiction between an educational success story and the growing need for simple community life; the contradiction between acceptance in respectable circles and the feeling of alienation and separation; the contradiction between speaking and lecturing about community and the loneliness of a highly individualized suburban existence; the contradiction between speaking more and more about religion and knowing God less and less. Parker lived these contradictions, and tested them with his wife and children in spite of the cautionary voices surrounding him. Living these contradictions brought him to insights, ideas and perspectives which could have been found in no other way.

This book is important not because it is written by a good scholar, but because it is written by a scholar who dared to wonder if his scholarship really led him to the truth. It is important not because it is written by a man who knows more than most people about the dynamics of community life, but because it is written by a man who gave up a large salary and moved away from a successful career to find community. It is important not because it is written by a man who has been a consultant to many on educational matters, but because it is written by a man who kept wondering if his own education didn't do him more harm than good and who gave much of his energy to a form of education not dominated by grades and degrees. It is not important because it is written by a man who knows the Bible well, but because it is written by a man who dared to let the Bible make radical claims on his own life and the lives of those he loves.

The way this book came about is the best testimony to its value. It came out of living the contradictions even when it was hard and painful to do so. This explains why the book does not offer one sustained argument; it contains six experiments in thinking which are all very radical in intent. I cannot read these pieces without wondering about my own life and without having to deal with my desire as well as resistance to move in the direction Parker points out.

The issues that Parker discusses are basic: solitude, community, social action, political responsibility, prayer and contemplation. They are raised in the context of the words of William Johnston: "Faith is the breakthrough into that deep realm of the soul which accepts paradox . . . with humility." Accepting paradox with humility is the spirit that binds the quite diverse pieces of this book together. And it is the spirit that makes this book worth reading.

Parker Palmer has taught me much over the years. He has given me some very helpful concepts to work with; he has shown me how to think clearly and concisely; he has introduced me to many inspiring people and books. But most of all, he has challenged me by his own decisions to keep moving to unknown fields without apprehension or fear. He has taught me to live boldly and freely. That our many hours together can now be shared with others through this book is a source of great joy to me.

I hope and pray that those who read these essays will sense the spirit in which they were written and thus be challenged as I have been to break out of illusions and compulsions and seek a new freedom.

HENRI J.M. NOUWEN

# 1

## In the Belly of a Paradox

### INTRODUCTION

In 1953, in his 12th year as a Trappist monk, Thomas Merton published a journal of his days called *The Sign of Jonas*. Fifteen years later, when I first read his preface, I knew I had been touched by a teacher and a friend:

> The sign Jesus promised to the generation that did not understand him was the "sign of Jonas the prophet"—that is, the sign of his own resurrection. The life of every . . . Christian is signed with the sign of Jonas because we all live by the power of Christ's resurrection. But I feel that my own life is especially sealed with this great sign . . . because like Jonas himself I find myself travelling toward my destiny in the belly of a paradox.[1]

Here is Merton's writing at its best, sturdy with religious conviction but laced with wit and fresh images of the religious life. That would have been enough for me, but I was drawn by substance as well as style, by the idea of life as a whale of a paradox!

Contradiction, paradox, the tension of opposites: These have always been at the heart of my experience, and I think I am not alone. I am tugged one way and then the other. My beliefs and my actions often seem at odds. My strengths are sometimes cancelled by my weaknesses. My self, and the world around me, seem more a study in dissonance than a harmony of the integrated whole.

More than once have I despaired at the corrosive effect of these contradictions on my "spiritual life." I had

15

thought that living spiritually required a resolution of all contraries and tensions before one could hope, as it were, to earn one's wings. But as I labored to remove the contradictions before presenting myself to God, my spiritual life became a continual preliminary attraction, never quite getting to the main event. I thought I was living in the spirit by railing against life's inconsistencies when, in fact, I was becoming more frustrated, more anxious, more withdrawn from those vital places in life where contradiction always lurks.

For me, there was light and liberation in Merton's image of life in the belly of a paradox. Perhaps one need not resolve life's contradictions single-handedly. Perhaps one could be swallowed up by paradox and still be delivered to the shores of one's destiny—even as was Jonah from the belly of the whale. Perhaps contradictions are not impediments to the spiritual life, but an integral part of it. Through them we may learn that the power for life comes from God, not from us.

Thomas Merton was well qualified to teach us about contradiction and paradox! He was a monk vowed to solitude and silence—who wrote more than sixty books and became an international figure in his own time. He withdrew from the pace and demands of worldly life to pray among Kentucky's wooded hills—and yet saw prophetically into racism and militarism and became patron saint of social activists. A Roman Catholic whose early writings are sometimes too parochial for our tastes—he became a universal religious figure, steeped in Taoism and Zen, claimed by some in the East to be an incarnate Buddha.

In the midst of his contradictions Merton found the grace of God, and that discovery is a gift to all of us whose lives are pulled between the poles. In the preface to a collection of his essays Merton writes:

I have had to accept the fact that my life is almost totally paradoxical. I have also had to learn gradually to get along without apologizing for the fact, even to myself. And perhaps this preface is an indication that I have not yet completely learned. No matter. It is in the paradox itself, the paradox which was and is still a source of insecurity, that I have come to find the greatest security. I have become convinced that the very contradictions in my life are in some ways signs of God's mercy to me; if only because someone so complicated and so prone to confusion and self-defeat could hardly survive for long without special mercy.[2]

In this essay I want to explore and celebrate some contradictions in Merton's thought and see what he has to teach us about our own.

## CONTRADICTION, PARADOX, AND THE LIFE OF THE SPIRIT

The contradictions of life are not accidental. Nor do they result from inept living. They are inherent in human nature and in the circumstances which surround our lives. We are, as the Psalmist says, "little less than God" but also "like the beasts that perish" (Ps 8:5; 49:12). Our highest insights and aspirations fail because we are encumbered by flesh which is too weak—or too strong. When we rise to soar on wings of spirit, we discover weights of need and greed tied to our feet. The things we seek consciously and with effort tend to evade us, while our blessings come quietly and unbidden. When we achieve what we most want, our pleasure in it often fades.

These contradictions of private life are multiplied over and over when we enter the world of work and politics. Here are a thousand factions competing for scarce resources. Here is a realm where values cancel each other out: How, for example, can we simultaneously have freedom and equality? In this arena vision yields to compromise, the law of collective survival. This is a self-negating world where even our finest achievements often yield negative by-products: Medical science lengthens human life only to increase starvation in some societies and draw out the agonies of aging in others.

Beyond the private and the public realms are contradictions we might call cosmic, which implicate even God! These are the religious conundrums which have bedeviled men and women for millennia. Why do the wicked flourish while the virtuous wither? How can there be evil in the universe if God is loving, all-knowing, and omnipotent? At every level our lives are stretched and torn between opposites which seem irreconcilable, discouraging, defeating.

Thomas Merton has helped me understand that the way we respond to contradiction is pivotal to our spiritual lives. The points at which we meet and reckon with contradiction are turning points at which we either enter or evade the mystery of God, the God who said: "I form light and create darkness, I make weal and create woe . . . ." (Is 45:7).

The spiritual journey sharpens and magnifies our sense of contradiction. And should it not be so? The wholeness of the Spirit contrasts dramatically with the brokenness of our persons and our world. The truth of the Spirit only highlights the untruths we are living. Indeed, the ultimate contradiction is the apparent opposition between God's light and our own shadowed lives.

For some of us the contrast between God and world is so great that we abandon the spiritual quest. We turn away from God's brilliance and walk in shadows because we do not wish to see ourselves in an unbecoming light. For others, the tension is resolved by disowning the dark world and trying to live in a bright but private realm. We hold the world at a distance and seek out situations which satisfy our need to stay "pure." In one way or another, we remove ourselves from the great dramas of life where God and world interact, where contradiction abounds.

But there is a third way to respond. A way beyond choosing either this pole or that. Let us call it "living the contradictions." Here we refuse to flee from tension but allow that tension to occupy the center of our lives. And why would anyone walk this difficult path? Because by doing so we may receive one of the great gifts of the spiritual life—*the transformation of contradiction into paradox.* The poles of either/or, the choices we thought we had to make, may become signs of a larger truth than we had even dreamed. And in that truth, our lives may become larger than we had ever imagined possible!

At this point I need to define my terms and begin to use them with more precision. A contradiction (says the *Oxford English Dictionary)* is a statement containing elements logically at variance with one another. A paradox is a statement which seems self-contradictory but on investigation may prove to be essentially true.

Many religious insights would be judged contradictions by the standards of normal logic. But by spiritual standards these insights contain paradoxical truth:

>—He who finds his life will lose it, and he who loses his life for my sake will find it (Mt 10:34).
>—Before I grasped Zen the mountains were nothing but mountains and the rivers nothing but rivers. When I got into Zen, the mountains were no longer mountains and the rivers no longer rivers. But when I understood Zen, the mountains were only mountains and the rivers only rivers (Zen saying).
>—Love is something if you give it away, you end up having more! (Popular song)

Spiritual truth will often seem self-contradictory when judged by the logic of the world. Where that logic wants to separate and divide, the spiritual eye looks for what Merton called life's "hidden wholeness," the underlying unity of all things. Logic assumes that there is no truth which

violates the rules devised by human mind. Faith assumes
that those rules become less and less useful as our questions grow deeper. The spiritual life proceeds in a kind of
trembling certainty that God's truth lies beyond all verities
of logic.

But a word or two of warning before I move on. By em-
phasizing the possibility of paradox, I do not intend to en-
dorse the popular view that all opposites are the same, that
there are no critical differences between true and false,
right and wrong. Such a view weakens the idea of paradox
whose truth comes only from the fact that the world is full
of very real opposites pulling vigorously against each
other. We appreciate paradox not by abandoning our
critical faculties but by sharpening them.

I have heard the term "paradox" used as if it were an in-
cantation which could magically remove life's tensions and
relieve us of responsibility for them. I have heard people
use the word to describe the gap between behavior and
belief as if the word itself would excuse the contradiction,
sanctify it, and allow us to forget about it. But that is what
Bonhoeffer called "cheap grace," and nothing could be
further from Merton's understanding or mine.

Our first need is not to release the tension, but to live the
contradictions, fully and painfully aware of the poles between which our lives are stretched. As we do so, we will be
plunged into paradox, at the center of which we will find
transcendence and new life. Our lives will be changed.
Both our beliefs and our actions will become more responsive to God's spirit. But this will happen only as we allow
ourselves to be engulfed by contradictions which God
alone can resolve. With Jonah, we will be delivered. But
first we will be swallowed into darkness.

Just as Thomas Merton helps us understand ourselves
through contradiction and paradox, so those principles
help us understand his thought. In hopes of achieving both

goals, I want to look at Merton's treatment of three topics: Marxism, Taoism, and the way of the cross. Though these may seem contradictory ways of life, Merton shows how the tensions among them open into deeper truth. I should caution the reader that my assessment of these matters, though rooted in Merton, grows out of my own thinking as well. I hope I have not contradicted anything the monk might have said. But if I have, may paradox abound!

## THE WAY OF MARXISM

Merton's interest in Marxism probably had several sources. The fact that many Christians regard Marxism as anathema doubtless appealed to that part of Merton which loved to explore "the other side" of everything. Merton, who entered the monastery in a mood of world-rejection, learned there to love the world, and one expression of his love was to keep informed about the political philosophy by which a majority of the world lives. But above all, Merton must have been attracted by the fact that contradiction was at the heart of Marx's own life and thought, as Merton points out in a passage which reveals the monk as well as Marx:

> Karl Marx would not work for his living, or even write for money. Yet he got Engels to write articles for him, which he sold to the New York *Tribune*. Engels practically supported Marx in England: Engels, who was one of the bosses in his father's capitalist firm in Manchester. Out of these contradictions springs the genial theory of alienation, and the humanism of labor. . . . Shall we on this account disbelieve everything he said? No, for he was a great diagnostician. He saw the disease of modern man, who has come to be ruled by things and by money, and by machines. . . . In any case, there is no point in judging the inner contradictions of Marx's life with an exaggerated severity. All men, especially all who have talent, tend to be

inconsistent. Their very struggle with their inconsistency
seeks an outlet and a solution in creative works. But what
is significant in Marx is that his analysis of society is a
keenly intuitive analysis of inconsistency. He is quick to
see the hidden contradictions in every ideology, every
social structure.[3]

According to Marx (who borrowed from Hegel) contradiction is the mainspring of history, the source of
historical movement. This process, called the dialectic,
moves through three stages. At any given moment, history
is dominated by a "thesis," or a dominant state of affairs.
But sooner or later opposition develops to that thesis, an
opposition called the "antithesis." Out of that tension a
new and higher state called a "synthesis" will emerge. But
then the synthesis becomes a thesis, a new contradiction
sets in, and the historical dynamic continues.

Marx believed that the dialectic always develops around
economic factors—that is, he believed that economic factors are the only real forces shaping and changing human
life. The contradictions which move history arise from the
different, and unequal, relations people have to the center
of economic power and privilege. In modern times, under
capitalism, the basic contradiction is easily described: A
few people are owners who control the economic power,
while the vast majority are workers who are controlled by
it. Under capitalism, then, the contradiction is one of
economic injustice. Many men and women are exploited
through hard work and low pay so that a few may grow
over-rich through no effort or virtue of their own. Marx
believed that this contradiction would eventually become a
conflict, with workers rising up against the owners in a
great revolution. The outcome of this collision of thesis
and antithesis would be a new synthesis—the classless
society, in which economic injustice is eradicated, in which
each gives according to ability and each takes according to
need.

Marx was explicit about the role of religion in all this: "Religion is the opiate of the people." Marx argued that religion served merely to justify economic injustice, to rationalize the difference between the haves and the havenots. Rich people believe that God has especially blessed them and that the poor somehow deserve their plight, while poor people hold a faith which promises a better life beyond this world, "pie in the sky when you die by-and-by." As Marx saw it, religion possesses no power for change toward justice, only the power to drug people into acceptance of an unjust *status quo.*

On the face of it, Marxism and Christianity seem to be as far apart as two ways of thinking can be. But contradictions tend to travel away from each other on great circles which come together again, and Merton knew that Marxism and Christianity, though beginning with very different assumptions about the nature of reality, come full circle in certain respects. Despite the fact that Marx denied God, Marxism reminds us of key elements in Christian faith which Christians have a bad habit of forgetting.

Marxism and Christianity converge in the idea that "religion is the opiate of the people," if by religion we mean its intellectual and institutional forms. Jesus, the prophets, and many mystics tried to give voice to the living experience of God against the dead forms of their times; Bonhoeffer even spoke about "religionless Christianity." The ministry of every authentic religious leader is to break people from their addiction to inauthentic forms of faith and lead them into dependence on the one, true, and living God. Marx's critique of religion in its institutional and intellectual forms is the stock-in-trade of every religious virtuoso.

A second convergence between Marxism and Christianity is in their common concern for the problems of the poor. Now, that claim could hardly be sustained on the

evidence of the affluent American church, for here we
have a primary illustration of how "religion" has become
an opiate: We have largely lost that passion for the poor
which so permeated Jesus' ministry. Marx was right. We
construe religion to justify ourselves, and the religion of
many middle-class Americans is designed to dull their sense
of justice and allow them to live complacently in the midst
of glaring economic contradictions. But when we read the
New Testament with a clear eye, we see how often
economics and salvation are linked: "Blessed are you
poor, for yours is the Kingdom of God" (Lk 6:20); ". . . it
is easier for a camel to go through the eye of a needle than
for a rich man to enter the Kingdom of God" (Mt 19:24).
If these are not the most oft-quoted passages of scripture
on Sunday morning, it is not because they lack prominence
in Jesus' view of things.

A third place where Marxism and Christianity converge
is in the idea of the classless society. One of the earliest
descriptions we have of a group in which each gave according to ability and took according to need is that passage in
Acts which describes the church of Pentecost: "And all
who believed were together and had all things in common;
and they sold their possessions and goods and distributed
them all, as any had need" (Acts 2:44-45). That church is
meant to be a sign of greater things to come, of a world in
which all will care for all. So there is a major parallel between Marxist and Christian *hope,* a parallel between the
classless society and the kingdom of God on earth. The
eradication of economic injustice, of hunger and
hopelessness is not the only mark of that kingdom, but it
is surely an essential one. Marx was steeped in the biblical
culture of messianic hope, a culture which proclaims that
men and women and children will someday be delivered
from the hateful relations of oppressor and oppressed.

A fourth convergence between Marxism and Christianity is fundamental and undergirds all the others. Both systems of thought and action assume that we are enslaved by a "false consciousness" of who we are, a false understanding of our origins and destiny as human beings. And both aim at shattering that false consciousness so that we may know the truth and the truth will set us free. Marx was primarily concerned to show people their bondage to economic powers and to point out that revolutionary class struggle is the road to liberation. Jesus decried our bondage to sin (including its economic varieties) and proclaimed the liberation available to us through God's justice and mercy. Though there are substantial differences between these diagnoses, the convergence remains in the midst of contradiction: Both Marxism and Christianity want to shatter our illusions with a vision of truth, and through the truth they want to win our liberation.

In each of these convergences, Marxism reveals something essential to Christianity, but something which has been obscured and forgotten through centuries of inattention and distortion. By pursuing the dialogue between Marxism and Christianity, Merton was able to develop a critical perspective on monastic life—a perspective which is not merely Marxist but stands on principles within the Christian tradition which Marxism helps to reveal. Such is the nature of a paradox: Apparently alien points of view can remind us of the inner truth of our own! I want to explore Merton's critique of monasticism here because it applies with force to all of us on spiritual paths, monks or not.

The challenge that Merton drew from Marxism and put to monastics can be summed up in two words: Justify yourself! In one of his talks to the novices, Merton reminds the would-be monks that every time they take a bite of food they depend on the labor of others for their very existence.[4] Even the monk who has "left the world" is not really out of the world; as long as he has to eat he is beholden to the world's labor. The question is, how do we make sure that these dependencies are not one-sided and exploitative? How do we live in fair exchange, so that what we consume is balanced out by what we produce? How can our spiritual labors be as useful to the people who feed us as their labors are to us?

These questions may annoy people who believe that our spiritual life, our relation to God, is an end in itself and thus needs no external justification. That is true—but only as one pole of a paradox! For it is equally true that "You will know them by their fruits" (Mt 7:20). This challenge seems especially important today when the popular spirituality is narcissistic, self-obsessed and self-indulgent. The religion of the American middle class sometimes seems to mock the Gospels; it aims at enhancing the self-esteem of persons who have material comfort while ignoring conditions of poverty and pestilence which deprive a whole class of people of life itself, let alone feelings of self-worth. What are the fruits of your spiritual life, and mine?

When Merton responds to the challenge to justify monastic life, he reveals his capacity to transcend thesis and antithesis. For, if he were to answer in a strictly Marxist mode, Merton would have to argue that the monastery should produce some useful material good. But Merton, who often carped at the monastery's obsession with making cheese (and who used to joke about "cheeses for Jesus"), does not take that route. Instead, he argues that the monastery must repay its debt to the world's labor by "producing people." The same obligation applies, I think, to every kind of spiritual endeavor.

But what does it mean to "produce people"? For Merton, the answer is simple: It means that monks must develop the capacity to love. Merton makes his point to the novices by using the image of "the heart":

> If I love God, I've got to love him with my heart. If I love
> him with my heart I've got to have a heart, and I've got to
> have it in my possession to give. One of the most difficult
> things in life today is to gain possession of one's heart in
> order to be able to give it. We don't have a heart to give.
> We have been deprived of these things, and the first step in
> the spiritual life is to get back what we have to give. . . .[5]

Here Merton points to a deep and vital convergence of
Marxism and Christianity. Where Marx spoke of the
alienation of labor, Merton speaks of the alienation of our
hearts. Where Marx argued that capitalism robbed people
of both the meaning and the benefits of their work, Merton argues that modern life robs us of our hearts. Here is
how Merton put it in his final talk, given just hours before
he died:

> The idea of alienation is basically Marxist, and what it
> means is that man living under certain economic condi-
> tions is no longer in possession of the fruits of his life. His
> life is not his. It is lived according to conditions determined
> by somebody else. I would say that on this particular
> point, which is very important indeed in the early Marx,
> you have a basically Christian idea. Christianity is against
> alienation. Christianity revolts against the alienated life.
> The whole *New Testament* is, in fact—and can be read by a
> Marxist-oriented mind as—a protest against religious
> alienation.[6]

What does it mean to be robbed of our hearts? For one
thing, it means that our ability to feel connected with
others, implicated in their lives, has been stolen from us,
for it is through our hearts that we feel solidarity with our
brothers and sisters. It is a common malady in modern
times, this inability to empathize with the stranger.
Whatever one may think of Marxist politics, one must
acknowledge that Marx had deep empathy for the plight of
the poor, the kind of empathy Jesus called for when he
said, ". . . as you did it to one of the least of these my
brethren, you did it to me" (Mt 25:40). But the conditions
of modern life have calloused so many hearts. We seem

unable to feel, unable to have our hearts broken by the fact
of children who are starving and parents who are unable to
provide. Our individualized way of life makes us feel alone
and unrelated; our competitive way of life makes us feel
that our gains must come at the expense of others, just as
their gains mean our loss. As Merton says, we don't have
possession of our hearts. They have been seized by concerns of self-preservation and self-enhancement, and by
the maintenance of institutions which serve these ends. If
we are to give our hearts we must get them back, and this is
the first task in the spiritual life. How strange that Marxism, which seems heartless to so many Christians, would
remind Merton that we must regain our hearts! Such is the
nature of contradiction as it deepens into paradox.

But to be in possession of our hearts is not simply to be
able to feel. Since the heart is an image for our whole being, we must also be able to translate feelings into action,
to work for the kingdom. And here is where Merton and
the Christian tradition diverge again from Marx, who
relied on the use of violence to overthrow the powers that
be. In Marx's mind, the contradictions of history led inevitably to violent confrontation, and only through the
warfare of the oppressed against the oppressors could the
classless society come to pass.

There is another theory of social action which also faces
the contradictions of history and yet comes to a quite different conclusion. The theory of nonviolent change is committed to the notion that beyond every conflict there is a
resolution, a synthesis, a common good, which will only be
obscured by violence, but which will be revealed by pa-
tience, dialogue, careful and prayerful consideration.
Since the contending parties are usually in no mood for
prayer, it is the task of the nonviolent mediator to stand
between the antagonists and by attitudes and actions serve
as a living guide to peaceful and creative change. The non-

violent mediator quite literally "lives the contradiction."

Thomas Merton was committed to nonviolence, and I turn now to one of its major sources in his life. Here we will see another of the many paradoxes which shaped Merton's thought. From Marxism, which is surely the major theory of action in modern times, Merton learned not about social change but about the spiritual affairs of the heart. His understanding of action draws deeply from Taoism, which is widely (though wrongly) understood to advocate retreat from the world, acceptance of what is given, and a passive way of life!

## THE WAY OF CHUANG TZU

*Wu wei* is the Chinese word for "non-action." It occurs often in *The Way of Chuang Tzu,* a Taoist classic which Merton translated through his own religious understanding. It is a strange word to find at the heart of an exploration of social action, but there it is, a paradox in all its glory! Here is a poem from the sage Chuang Tzu which gives some sense of how *wu wei* is used:

> Fishes are born in water,
> Man is born in Tao.
> If fishes, born in water,
> Seek the deep shadow
> Of pond and pool,
> All their needs
> Are satisfied.
> If man, born in Tao,
> Sinks into the deep shadow
> Of non-action *(wu wei)*
> To forget aggression and concern,
> He lacks nothing
> His life is secure.
>
> Moral: "All the fish needs
> Is to get lost in water.
> All man needs is to get lost
> in Tao."[7]

On the face of it, the poem seems to counsel a return to the womb, a withdrawal from the problems and pressures of society for the sake of individual happiness. It sounds all too much like the new narcissism and seems to contradict the Marxist impulse toward social engagement. If we are to see how this contradiction becomes paradox, and thus understand why Merton was so deeply drawn to the religious experience of the East, we must first understand Merton's critique of social action as it is commonly defined and practiced.

Merton became the patron saint of social activists because he spoke so clearly to their condition. He understood what it means to be driven by the desire to hasten the coming of the kingdom:

> Douglas Steere remarks very perceptively that there is a pervasive form of contemporary violence to which the idealist fighting for peace by nonviolent methods most easily succumbs: activism and overwork. The rush and pressure of modern life are a form, perhaps the most common form, of its innate violence. To allow oneself to be carried away by a multitude of conflicting concerns, to surrender to too many demands, to commit oneself to too many projects, to want to help everyone in everything is to succumb to violence. More than that, it is cooperation in violence. The frenzy of the activist neutralizes his work for peace. It destroys his own inner capacity for peace. It destroys the fruitfulness of his own work, because it kills the root of inner wisdom which makes work fruitful.[8]

Note that Merton is troubled not only by the cost of activism to the activist. He is also concerned about the cost society pays for a type of social action which turns out to be violence in disguise. In his essay on "Contemplation in a World of Action" he makes this clear:

> He who attempts to act and do things for others or for the world without deepening his own self-understanding, freedom, integrity and capacity to love, will not have anything to give others. He will communicate to them nothing but the contagion of his own obsessions, his ag-

gressiveness, his ego-centered ambitions, his delusions about ends and means, his doctrinaire prejudices and ideas. There is nothing more tragic in the modern world than the misuse of power and action to which men are driven by their own Faustian misunderstandings and misapprehensions.[9]

Those "Faustian misunderstandings and misapprehensions" are the core of our problem, and Taoism aims at rooting them out. Social action requires power, but whenever we humans come close to power, trouble often follows. We think we want power as a means to other ends, but holding power tends to become an end in itself. We think we want power to work for the common good, but are tempted to use it for purposes of self-promotion and self-enhancement. Not only do these tendencies deflect our action from its original aims, they often lead to acts that are simply counterproductive. Taoism thus serves to criticize and clarify our action; Chuang Tzu wants to show up our conception of power for the delusion it is and guide us toward a right relation with true power. Only by moving with Tao, or the Way, or the will of God, can we hope to bring peace on earth.

The way in which our illusions about power defeat our best-intended actions is illustrated by Chuang Tzu's poem "The Need to Win":

> When an archer is shooting for nothing
> He has all his skill.
> If he shoots for a brass buckle
> He is already nervous.
> If he shoots for a prize of gold
> He goes blind
> Or sees two targets—
> He is out of his mind!
> His skill has not changed. But the prize
> Divides him. He cares.
> He thinks more of winning
> Than of shooting—
> And the need to win
> Drains him of power.[10]

Note that the poem does not counsel against winning. Instead, it is a paradoxical counsel on how to win! It says that the only way to victory is to forget about victory, to be indifferent to it. When Taoism tells us not to care, it does not mean that we should be indifferent to the many needs around us, but that we should not let our desire to meet these needs drain us of the power to do so. Every thoughtful activist knows how the desire for success and the fear of failure can pervert social action, and even lead to fraud, with the activist settling for the mere appearance of victory rather than persisting for deep and lasting change. When we get caught in the dualism of winning and losing we become possessed by false and misleading powers.

That paradox is acceptable within the Christian tradition, I think; it reminds us of Jesus' counsel that one who seeks life will lose it, but one who loses life in God will find it. But Taoism pushes us even further by insisting that our actions must transcend not only the polarity of win and lose, but also the polarity of good and evil. And here Western sensibilities are offended. Here we want to say that this paradox business has gone far enough! For surely if there is any motive force for right action, or any plumb line against which our actions can be judged, it is in ethics, in the distinction between right and wrong. What D.T. Suzuki writes about the Christian reaction to Zen can also be said of our response to Taoism:

> The Zen-man . . . who talks of going beyond the dualism of good and evil, of right and wrong, of life and death, of truth and falsehood, will most likely be a subject of suspicion. The idea of social values deeply ingrained in Western minds is intimately connected with religion so that they are led to think religion and ethics are one and the same, and that religion can ill-afford to relegate ethics to a position of secondary importance.[11]

But religion is not the same as ethics. In fact, it can be

argued that as religion declines, ethics ascends to take its place. From Taoism we learn that religion is a mode of connectedness with the creative force of life. When one is thus connected one's actions are responsive to the needs of life; when one is truly part of the body of humankind, then a hurt in one part of the body will trigger remedial action in the other parts.

But when we lose this connectedness with life, with one another, then we need a code of ethics to tell us what we ought to do. When life is fragmented and disconnected, our organic relations with one another are replaced by "oughts." And eventually these oughts, these ethics, become an abstract system of thought far removed from human needs, a creed to be defended rather than a relation to be lived. The spiritual life teaches wholeness, integration with all being, and out of that wholeness come true power and true action. Life beyond ethics is no libertine life, no denial of moral discipline; on the contrary, to live a life of true connectedness is a spiritual discipline of the highest order. John Middleton Murry has said it well, I think: "For the good man to realize that it is better to be whole than to be good is to enter on a strait and narrow path compared to which his previous rectitude was flowery license."[12]

A number of Chuang Tzu's poems portray the "well-connected" life, the life through which the Tao flows unimpeded into creative activity. One of my favorites is "The Woodcarver":

Khing, the master carver, made a bell stand
Of precious wood. When it was finished,
All who saw it were astounded. They said it must be
The work of spirits.
The Prince of Lu said to the master carver:
"What is your secret?"

Khing replied: "I am only a workman:
I have no secret. There is only this:
When I began to think about the work you commanded

I guarded my spirit, did not expend it
On trifles, that were not to the point.
I fasted in order to set
My heart at rest.
After three days fasting,
I had forgotten gain and success.
After five days
I had forgotten praise or criticism.
After seven days
I had forgotten my body
With all its limbs.

"By this time all thoughts of your Highness
And of the court had faded away.
All that might distract me from the work
Had vanished.
I was collected in the single thought
Of the bell stand.

"Then I went to the forest
To see the trees in their own natural state.
When the right tree appeared before my eyes,
The bell stand also appeared in it, clearly, beyond doubt.
All I had to do was to put forth my hand
And begin.

"If I had not met this particular tree
There would have been
No bell stand at all.

"What happened?
My own collected thought
Encountered the hidden potential in the wood;
From this live encounter came the work
Which you ascribe to the spirits."[13]

For me, that poem has implications for action which are
endlessly rich. Let me draw out only a few. First, the
wood-carver, as Merton comments, "does not simply proceed according to certain fixed rules and external standards."[14] In our age, which is so dominated by method
and technique, this comes near to being heresy! But deep
down we know that mastery in any realm goes beyond

rules and methods (just as truly responsive action goes beyond ethics). Instead of rules the great artist follows the spirit, the internal flow, the nature of the thing at hand. This is the way of greatness whether we are speaking of woodcarving, music, or human relations: It is based on a deep mutuality between the carver and the tree, the pianist and the music, or between persons. It is not based on a code.

Second, this mutuality can be achieved only through discipline. It is not incidental that the wood-carver fasted before beginning his work—let fasting stand for all those disciplines by which we attain (in Merton's words) "detachment, forgetfulness of results, and abandonment of all hope of profit."[15] Only through such disciplines can we transcend those anxieties about self and success which distort our actions. Only through such disciplines can we discern the intrinsic nature of the problem or persons to whom our action relates.

Third, the action of "The Woodcarver" requires a belief that things and people do have a "nature"; that is, limits and potentials. The modern mind does not hold this belief. Instead our culture teaches that all things from trees to people are infinitely changeable, malleable, plastic, and can assume whatever shape machine or method can create. Today a bell stand would be made from whatever tree is available (within the limits of economic feasibility) and produced by machine. If we want to change our human shape, physical or psychological, there are a variety of technologies which promise to do so. Most of our social action is based on this assumption, I think: that people can be seduced or compelled into whatever form fits the activist's conception of how things "ought" to be.

The wood-carver's message is clearly different. Here, true action, effective action, action that is full of grace, beauty and results, is action based on discernment of and

respect for the nature of the other. The reason is simple:
Only through such a relationship to the rest of reality can
our action flow with the action of the Tao. Only so can we
be channels for real power. Oh, we can make bell stands
any way we wish. We can hack and hew through forests
with no regard for the nature of the wood. We can produce
a stand that will hold a bell without bothering about Tao.
But we do so at great cost to the world and to ourselves.
Not only do we endanger our own survival when we misuse
and abuse the forests, but we also deprive our lives of
quality. So it is with much of our social action, action
which does not respect the nature of the other, action
which depends on human power and is perverted by
human pride. Through Taoism, Merton learned another
image of action. It is one which we need to know in our
own strained and frantic time.

Although Taoism stands on premises quite different
from Merton's Christianity, and seems to contradict Christian tradition at key points (as in the devaluation of ethics),
the more deeply we pursue the contradictions the more the
paradox comes clear. For the Taoist image of action has
much in common with the images of the New Testament.
The idea that success is achieved by not worrying about
success intersects the notion that we find our lives by losing
them. The idea that we should act without fear of the consequences finds its counterpart in Jesus' counsel "do not
be anxious about tomorrow" (Mt 6:34). And the Taoist
notion that we must empty ourselves to serve as channels
for the Tao is echoed in the life of Jesus—he who re-
nounced all worldly power, he who "emptied himself" and
"became obedient unto death, even death on a cross," so
that God's power could be shown (Phil 2:7,8).

But still the contradiction persists, and the mention of
the cross reminds us why. The man or woman of Tao is
always portrayed as the invisible person, the person who

attracts no attention and encounters no opposition. In the words of one poem:

> If you can empty your own boat
> Crossing the river of the world,
> No one will oppose you,
> No one will seek to harm you.[16]

And yet, in Christian tradition, the person who embodies God's word is the person who ends up on the cross. Opposition, harm, indeed betrayal, are, in the Christian view, potential consequences of "speaking truth to power." So, another contradiction! And one that was pivotal to Merton's life. For wherever his thought took him, through Marxism, Taoism and much more, the cross remained his central symbol and reality.


## THE WAY OF THE CROSS

The cross is, first, a historical fact, and it reminds us of one of history's major contradictions. Throughout the human story men and women have yearned for truth and goodness to touch their lives. But when these appear among us in human form, we are so threatened that we murder the one who fulfills our wish.

So the historical cross is also a symbol of contradictions. Its very structure suggests the oppositions of life—left and right, up and down. It symbolizes the way we are pulled between this person and that, between our conflicting obligations on life's "horizontal" plane. And the cross gives mute testimony of the way we are stretched upon the "vertical" dimension of life, between the demands of the divine and the fears of flesh. To walk the way of the cross is to be impaled upon contradictions, torn by opposition and tension and conflict.

And yet the way of the cross is also the way toward peace, toward the center where contradictions converge.

The cross speaks of the greatest paradox of all: That to live we have to die. To walk the way of the cross, to allow one's life to be torn by contradiction and swallowed up in paradox, is to live in the reality of resurrection, in the sign of Jonah. For the cross overcomes all contradictions. In symbol and in reality the crossing point is a point of transformation.

Let us see how the way of the cross transforms the insights Merton gained from the ways of Marx and Chuang Tzu. From his encounters with Marxism, Merton drew the paradoxical reminder that Christians must regain their alienated hearts in order to give them. Marxism, for all its materialism and atheism, begins in profound sympathy for the wretched of the earth, a sympathy which has been largely lost in affluent Christian circles. We are afraid to recover our hearts, afraid we will feel too much and be overwhelmed with pain. We fear the example of Jesus, that "man of sorrows, and acquainted with grief" (Is 53:3).

The problem with Marxism is not that it fails to feel pain, but that it has no way to transform that pain into a creative force. Instead, Marxism allows pain to pursue its natural and inevitable course toward anger, violence and self-multiplication. Suffering, unmediated and unalloyed, has only one outcome: more of the same. It may enlarge within the person who suffers, or that person may pass it on to others in a futile attempt at personal relief. The natural economy of suffering requires a continual inflation of the currency.

Thus, Marx's prescription for a suffering society calls for violent revolution followed by a "dictatorship" of the working class. Somehow, these steps are supposed to lead to a society of equity and peace. But one knows that the pain will persist. We have no reason to believe that change by violence and dictatorship foreshadows anything other than more of the same. At best the Marxist revolution might cause oppressor and oppressed to switch roles (and there would be grim justice in that). But Marxism has no means of transforming pain into peace.

In contrast, the cross signifies that pain stops here. The way of the cross is a way of absorbing pain, not passing it on; a way which transforms pain from destructive impulse into creative power. When Jesus accepted the cross, his death became a channel for the redeeming power of love. When we accept the crosses and contradictions in our lives, we allow that same power to flow. When we give our hearts to the world, our hearts will be broken. But they are broken open to become channels for a love greater than our own. Only as pain is transformed by love will the real revolution come, the revolution which promises to take us toward the peaceable kingdom.

With its emphasis on suffering, the way of the cross may be misunderstood as masochistic, especially in an age so desperately in search of pleasure. But the suffering of which Jesus spoke is not that which unwell people create for themselves. Instead, it is the suffering already present in the world which we can either ignore or identify with. If pain were not real, if it were not the lot of so many, the way of the cross would be pathological. But in our world, with its hungry and homeless and hopeless, it is pathological to live as if pain did not exist. The way of the cross means letting that pain carve one's life into a channel through which the healing stream of the spirit can flow to a world in need.

That stream recalls Taoism, "the watercourse way," whose aim is the same as Christianity: to bring our beings and our actions into the flow of a power which is beyond all names. But Taoism seems to say that once we enter the stream we float along in ease, while Christianity insists that the stream is full of obstacles and dangers, that the flow of the spirit will bring us to the cross. Small wonder that

Taoism has had such appeal in the West where we endlessly look for an easy way out (and where we casually ignore the rigor and discipline inherent in the culture from which Taoism comes). Small wonder that Christian faith is more often preached than practiced!

But if the stream of spirit brings us to the cross, it also takes us beyond. The way of the cross is finally a way not of despair but of joy. If Jesus was "a man of sorrows, and acquainted with grief" he was also the one who said "my yoke is easy, and my burden is light" (Mt 11:30). For what we lose on the cross is the burden of falsehood and illusion. What lives beyond the cross is the uplifting power of love. The great paradox of the crucifixion is Christ's victory over the illusion that death is supreme. The paradox of our own crossing points is that pain kills illusion so that truth can bring joy.

The way of the cross reminds us that despair and disillusionment are not dead ends but signs of impending resurrection. Losing our illusions is painful because illusions are the stuff we live by. But God is the great iconoclast, constantly smashing these idols on which we depend. Beyond illusion lies a fuller truth which can be glimpsed only as our falsehoods die. Only as we have the faith to live fully in the midst of these painful contradictions will we experience resurrection and the transformation of our lives.

Merton spoke often of two illusions which must die on the cross if we are to become channels of the Spirit. The first is our false sense of self, for that self separates us from God and from each other, and such separation is the basic form of sin. This is the self full of pride and pretense, the self which tries to control life for its own benefit. This is the self which wants to resolve all contradictions by ignoring or denying them, the self which hopes to live without ambiguity or pain. This is the idolatrous self, the self which thinks it is God and wants to create the world in its own image. This false self must die if we are to live, but since it is the only self we know we struggle to keep it alive and often lose it only when we are overwhelmed by the cross.

Here, as everywhere, there is a paradox! In order to lose one's ego one must have an ego to lose. There seems to be a need for each person to build up a false sense of self, of difference from others, before the spiritual struggle to become part of the "hidden wholeness" can begin. And deeper still, there is the paradox that not until the false self dies does the true self come into being. The destruction of ego does not mean a loss of personhood. The individual in whom the false self has been shattered is not a faceless cipher or a pale imitation of the real thing. Instead, this is a person in whom flow all the currents of life, human and divine.

The second illusion which must die on the cross is our false conception of the world. The two illusions are related since much of the false self is built around our notion of what "the world" wants and demands of us. Merton was especially sensitive to our images of the world since he saw monasteries filled with men motivated by world rejection. He fought this tendency in the religious life, this temptation to see the world as evil and the spiritual life as pure. As always, he insisted that we live out the contradictions and discover the underlying paradox.

In one of his talks to the novices, Merton chides them for thinking of the world as an independent entity, a thing " out there," capable of imposing demands and conditions on their lives.[17] It is wrong, he says, to come to the monastery in order to escape the world so conceived, for the conception is false. The world, Merton insists, does not begin at the monastery gatehouse. It is *within* each one of us. We are the world! The world will have power over us only insofar as we grant it that power. The world will be a force "out there" constraining and diverting our energies only if we grant that illusion reality and let it govern our lives.

Again, the pain of living the contradictions is partly the pain of having our illusions shattered. We construct the illusion of a powerful world "out there" because it lets us off the hook: "The world made me do it." When the contradictions of life show us how incoherent and chaotic that world really is, we are loath to give up our excuse. It is somehow more comforting to believe that the world is a monolith which forces us into certain ways of life than to accept the fact that we have the freedom to respond fully to God's will.

Freedom, finally, is what the cross is all about. After the tension, after the suffering, after the death, and after the resurrection comes freedom. As Merton put it, "The cross is . . . the only liberation from . . . servitude to the illusions which are packaged and sold as 'the world.' "[18] The cross liberates us from the idea that the world is "out there," over and against us; the experience of the cross reveals that the world is in us, in both its glory and its shame. So we can see, in Merton's words, "that the world is a matter of interpenetration and is not something absolute like a brick structure. The world isn't something we have to adjust to. It's something we adjust."[19] Since the world is in us, we are responsible for the world; and the shape the world takes depends on how we live our lives. The cross brings freedom, but with that freedom comes responsibility, or "the ability to respond" to the claims of justice.

And the liberation the cross gives us goes further yet. Not only are we freed from illusion and freed to respond; we are also freed in the knowledge that the world is redeemed by a God who suffers contradictions with us. As long as we see the world as unredeemed, we will want to redeem it ourselves. The consequences of that impossible expectation are well known: frustration, anger, impotence, guilt and despair. But in the light of the cross we can see the world and ourselves in a new way. For God is already at work here, suffering brokenness but always offering the gift of reconciliation. By accepting the cross in our own lives, we will be brought into the stream of God's mighty work and given the gift of hope.

So, in the manner of paradox, we come full circle. By living the contradictions we will be brought through to hope, and only through hope will we be empowered to live life's contradictions. How do we break into this circle which goes round and round with no apparent point of entry? Someday, far out at sea, heading away from the place where the Lord has called us and lost in contradictions, we will be swallowed by grace and find ourselves, with Jonah, with Thomas Merton, and with all the saints, traveling toward our destiny in the belly of a paradox.

## FOOTNOTES

1. Thomas Merton, *The Sign of Jonas* (NY: Harcourt, Brace and Co., 1953), p. 11.
2. Thomas P. McDonnell, ed., *A Thomas Merton Reader* (Garden City, NY: Image Books, 1974), p. 16.
3. Thomas Merton, *Conjectures of a Guilty Bystander* (NY: Doubleday and Co., 1966), pp. 12-13.
4. Thomas Merton, "Conscience of a Christian Monk," cassette tape produced by Electronic Paperbacks, 1972.
5. *Ibid.*
6. Thomas Merton, *The Asian Journal* (NY: New Directions, 1973), pp. 335-336.
7. Thomas Merton, *The Way of Chuang Tzu* (NY: New Directions, 1969), p. 65.
8. *Conjectures of a Guilty Bystander,* p. 73.
9. Thomas Merton, *Contemplation in a World of Action* (NY: Doubleday and Co., 1971), p. 164.
10. *The Way of Chuang Tzu,* p. 107.

11. Thomas Merton, *Zen and the Birds of Appetite* (NY: New Directions, 1968), pp. 103-104.
12. Quoted in Elizabeth Watson, *This I Know Experimentally* (Phila.: Friends General Conference, 1977), p. 16.
13. *The Way of Chuang Tzu,* pp. 110-111.
14. *Ibid.,* p. 31.
15. *Ibid.*
16. *Ibid.,* p. 114.
17. "Conscience of a Christian Monk."
18. *Ibid.*
19. *Ibid.*
All biblical quotations are from the Revised Standard Version.

# 2

## The Stations of the Cross: A Meditation

Among Catholic Christians there is an ancient tradition involving the "stations of the cross," each station corresponding to a key point in Jesus' journey to Calvary. One can find these stations portrayed in carved wood or stained glass along the passageways of parish churches. Here the faithful walk, pause, and pray, remembering Christ's sacrifice, opening themselves to the special insight which each station represents. There is the point at which Jesus falls: at which Simon of Cyrene carries the cross for Jesus; at which Jesus meets his mother; at which Jesus is nailed to the cross. Each point is full of portent and power for those who have eyes to see and ears to hear.

It seems to me there is another series of "stations of the cross," stations which represent not steps on an outward journey but moments of an inner movement as we live our lives through death toward resurrection. I want to write about five such moments which come from my inward experience of this way of life: I call them recognition, resistance, acceptance, affirmation, and liberation. This inward way of the cross does not always proceed in that order, and once one has passed through the five stations, the journey is not finished: It will recur again and again. This process goes on in our lives whether we acknowledge it or not: talking about it will neither prevent it nor make it easier. But by speaking of these inner stations of the cross perhaps we will grow in awareness of the path we are on, grow in faith and hope about its destination.

## RECOGNITION

First of all, recognition: The cross calls us to recognize that the heart of human experience is neither consistency nor chaos, but contradiction. In our century we have been beguiled by the claim of consistency, by the theory that history is moving toward the resolution of all problems, by the false hope that comes from groundless optimism that all works together for good. And then, when this claim has been discredited by tragic events, we have been assaulted by theories of chaos, by prophets of despair who claim that everything can be reduced to the random play of forces beyond all control, of events which lack inherent meaning.

But the cross symbolizes that beyond naive hope and beyond meaningless despair lies a structure of dynamic contradictions in which our lives are caught. The cross represents the way in which the world contradicts God: We yearn for light and truth and goodness to appear among us, but when they come in human form the world grows fearful and kills the incarnation. But then, the cross represents the way in which God contradicts the world: No matter how often the world says "no," God is present with an eternal "yes," bringing light out of darkness, hope out of despair, life out of death.

The very structure of the cross symbolizes these contradictions. Its arms reach left and right, up and down, signifying the way life pulls us between the conflicting claims of person against person, the conflicting claims of life human and life divine. And yet, the arms of the cross converge at the center, symbolizing the way in which God can act in our lives to overcome conflict, to unify the opposition, to contradict the contradictions! The cross calls us to recognize that reality has a cruciform shape.

Loren Eiseley tells a story which helps me feel the power of recognizing life's contradictions. That great naturalist once spent time in a seaside town called Costabel and, plagued by his lifelong insomnia, spent the early morning hours walking the beach. Each day at sunrise he found townspeople combing the sand for starfish which had washed ashore during the night, to kill them for commercial purposes. It was, for Eiseley, a sign, however small, of all the ways the world says no to life.

But one morning Eiseley got up unusually early, and discovered a solitary figure on the beach. This man, too, was gathering starfish, but each time he found one alive he would pick it up and throw it as far as he could out beyond the breaking surf, back to the nurturing ocean from which it came. As days went by Eiseley found this man embarked on his mission of mercy each morning, seven days a week, no matter the weather.

Eiseley named this man "the star thrower," and in a moving meditation he writes of how this man and his pre-dawn work contradicted everything that Eiseley had been taught about evolution and the survival of the fittest. Here on the beach in Costabel the strong reached down to save, not crush, the weak. And Eiseley wonders: Is there a star thrower at work in the universe, a God who contradicts death, a God whose nature (in the words of Thomas Merton) is "mercy within mercy within mercy"?

That story is rich in meaning for me. It offers an image of a God who threw the stars and throws them still. It speaks of how ordinary men and women can participate in God's enveloping mercy. And it suggests a vocation that each of us could undertake on our inward way of the cross: To recognize, to identify and lift up those moments, those acts, those people, those stories which contradict the ways in which the world says no to life.

That is what I mean by calling the first station on this inward way of the cross "recognition." To recognize the cruciform nature of reality is to see that the world is not monolithic, that things are not locked in place, that God is always moving among and within us contradicting the trend of antilife no matter how strong that trend may be. These contradictions may be few in number, but that does not matter. They become transforming when we recognize their superior reality, when we live in such a way as to make that reality manifest and abundant. The world is full of unlove, but if you have once been loved, you can live in the power of that moment and make it multiply.

I like to think of Christians as star throwers. I like to think of those who have stood at the shoreline of history, stood against the surf and the tide, and against all futility have reached down to affirm life, no matter how small and insignificant its form. How futile and foolish is the commitment to peace against the incessant evolution of war. And yet by standing in that futile and foolish place we contradict the course of social evolution. And by living the contradiction we participate in the power and hope of Christ's cross.

We are called to live the contradiction. Let me paraphrase the poet Rilke who, in his *Letters to a Young Poet,* wrote so movingly about "living the questions":

> Be patient toward all that is unresolved in your heart. . . .
> Try to love the contradictions themselves. . . . Do not now
> seek the resolutions, which cannot be given because you
> would not be able to live them, and the point is to live
> everything. Live the contradictions now. Perhaps you will
> then gradually, without noticing it, live along some distant
> day into the resolutions.

We are called to live the contradictions. We shall do so only as we recognize that reality has a cruciform shape, that contradiction is the heart of the way of the cross.


## RESISTANCE

The second station on this inward way of the cross I call resistance. It is not easy to be a star thrower, to stand against tides. There is much in our human nature that resists living the contradictions; much in us that tries to avoid tension, avoid life torn between the poles, avoid living on the cross. Though I abhor war, I continue to pay war taxes; I resist life on that particular cross. But in that failure, I am caught in yet another tension, impaled on yet another cross, torn between my own convictions and my inability to act them out.

I have come to believe that our resistance to such crosses, our resistance to God's will, is itself an aspect of the cruciform nature of reality. If we can recognize it as such, then our resistance, our tendency to contradict God, will generate great energy for life. By living fully in those tensions, neither denying nor ignoring them, we will be pulled open to the power of the Spirit.

I see this power illustrated in scripture, and especially in the Old Testament. The Old Testament is full of people resisting God: trying to trick God, to outwit God, to fly in the face of God's commands, to outdo God in the haggling of the marketplace. I like that because it humanizes the spiritual life. It assumes that God is a person who can be dragged into the human struggle. How often in our secular piety we treat God as an abstract principle who cannot enter the realities of the flesh! In doing so we deprive ourselves of a great source of energy for life—I mean a God who contends with us, as the angel wrestled with Jacob.

I believe it is God's will that I devote my whole self to the establishment of peace on earth. But how I struggle against that will! How I try to bargain with God, arguing that other claims on my life must be honored too: the claims of family, of career, of limited time and energy, of my prudent fears about the consequences of responding too fully to what the Lord requires. But as I live in that resistance, as I acknowledge it and confess it to myself and others, slowly my life is pulled open. As I live in the tension created by my fear of confronting war taxes, slowly my life is pulled open to other ways in which I can witness for peace. I look within my family, and find ways of living in harmony. I look at my career, and find ways of using my gifts toward the creation of a peaceable kingdom. My very resistance, my contention with God, stretches me to discover what I *can* do to witness to the light. This is one reason to attend to our resistance, to stay with it until it opens us to something new.

There is another reason to trust our resistance to the cross, for some crosses are false, not given by God, but placed upon us by a heedless world and received by an unhealthy part of ourselves. Christian tradition has too many examples of masochism masquerading as the way of the cross. And the church is full of people who submit all too easily to injustices which ought to be fought. So we have the problem of distinguishing valid crosses from invalid ones, crosses which lead toward the centerpoint from crosses which lead to desolation. I do not know of any abstract principles by which the one can be told from the other. Perhaps our natural resistance is as good a test as any. Resist any cross that comes your way. Boldly become a pole of opposition; live the contradiction. The false crosses will fall away, while those we must accept will stay there in the middle of our lives, pulling right and left, up and down, until they pull us open to our true center, a center where we are one with God, a center which we find only on the way of the cross.


## ACCEPTANCE

First recognition, then resistance, and now the third station on this inward way of the cross: acceptance. Few of us are so spiritually fulfilled that we can accept the crosses we are given in simple obedience. So another reason to resist a cross is that by resisting we become so worn down, so flattened out, so drained of energy and emptied of fight, that the only thing left is to accept!

The idea that acceptance follows resistance is confirmed by Elisabeth Kubler-Ross in her study of the stages of dying. She describes how the dying person first goes through denial, then anger, then bargaining, then depression, before finally reaching acceptance. Of course, denial, anger, bargaining and depression are all forms of resistance; we see them not only in cases of terminal illness, but in virtually all our relations with life. But after we have run out of resistance, then comes acceptance, acceptance of the cross.

This parallel with Kubler-Ross' work is powerful for me because the way of the cross is always a way of dying. On the cross our false dependencies are taken from us. On the cross our illusions are destroyed. On the cross our small self dies so that true self, the God self, can emerge. On the cross, we give up the fantasy that we are in control, and the death of this fantasy is central to acceptance.

The cross, above all, is a place of powerlessness. Here is the final proof that our own feeble powers can no more alter the stream of life than a magnet can pull down the moon. Here is the death of the ego, the death of the self that insists on being in charge, the self that is continually attempting to impose its own limited version of order and righteousness on the world.

But again, the cross contradicts itself. For the powerlessness of the cross, if it is fully entered, leads us to a place of power. This is the great mystery at the heart of Christian faith, at the heart of the person of Jesus, of Gandhi, of Martin Luther King, Jr.: The power of powerlessness. Or is it such a mystery after all? As long as

my center is occupied with the marshalling of my own feeble powers, there will be no space for God's power to flow
through me. As long as I am in my own way, I will not live
in the power of God's way.

Here is how Paul speaks of this moment of acceptance in
Jesus' crucifixion and ours: "In your minds you must be
the same as Christ Jesus: his state was divine, yet he did
not cling to his equality with God but *emptied* himself to
assume the condition of a slave, and became as men are;
and being as all men are he was humbler yet, even to accepting death, death on a cross."

Emptiness is a key word in describing the experience of
acceptance. And again, I find confirmation in the work of
Elisabeth Kubler-Ross, who says that the stage of acceptance in a dying person "should not be mistaken for a happy stage. It is almost void of feelings." Perhaps many of us
have had that sense, when we have finally accepted a difficult reality and there is simply a hole inside us, not a raw
place or a sinking space but a simple emptiness. So often it
is in such moments that a larger power flows through our
lives, through the space which has been emptied in us by
acceptance.

I have had that experience in teaching when I struggle to
plan a class, but work as I might nothing seems right; so I
finally give up, yield to my own inability, walk into class
feeling empty and unprepared—and in that state am
somehow able to be an open conduit for truth to flow between me and my students. Those are the times the
students say how good it was—not the times when I am
filled with plans which do not yield to the power of the
Spirit!

Jesus on the cross emptied himself so that God might
enter in. When we accept a cross, a void is created in us, a
void which is filled by the One whose creations begin in

nothing. In our powerlessness we are given the power of the Spirit life.

## AFFIRMATION

The fourth station on this inward way of the cross is affirmation. The cross becomes most powerful in our lives when we can go beyond acceptance to say, with confidence and hope and joy: This cross is mine. It is given to me by God. It is the way to larger life, the way to community with my brothers and sisters, with my God.

The way of the cross may seem a lonely way. But—and here is another contradiction—by walking that lonely way we find one another. The community we seek will not come because we want it or go after it. That community will come as we are willing to shoulder one another's burdens, pick up one another's crosses, and in the process find ourselves part of a gathered people where "the yoke is easy and the burden is light" because we share it with one another and with God.

It is not easy for us to think of affirming the cross with joy. But I know of no greater joy than the joy of community, than feeling at one and at home with one another. That joy will come only as we are willing to suffer the crossing points which lie at the heart of every relationship. Community means sharing and even creating one another's contradictions. Community means causing each other pain; even the easiest and most nurturing relationship will someday know the pain of separation. So if we want the joy of community, of relatedness, we must not only accept but affirm the experience of the cross.

We live in a time which some have called "the Me Decade," others "the new narcissism," a time when the pursuit of self-satisfaction has sometimes created an adult who seems almost autistic. There is much in our culture which has devalued community, which wants to keep relationships within safe bounds of mutual pleasure and comfort. The way of the cross cuts through the illusion that such relations bear any resemblance to real life by reminding us that true joy is found on the other side of shared suffering.

When I think about the people with whom I have the deepest sense of community, I think of people who have been able to share with me their contradictions, their brokenness—thus allowing me to share mine. When we present ourselves to the world as smooth and seamless we allow each other no way in, no way into life together. But as we acknowledge and affirm that the cross is the shape of our lives, we open a space within us where community can occur. And in that empty space, in that solitude at the center of the cross, the One who created us whole makes us whole again. And that is reason for affirmation, cause for joy!

If we are to affirm the cross, receive it with joy, we must somehow see that at its deepest reaches the cross is not only a tragic symbol but a comic one as well: that in the cross the tragic and the comic are constantly crossing paths. For contradiction is the stuff of which great comedy is made. A comedy builds as you follow the logic of a situation rigorously when zap! a totally illogical event occurs. A comic situation is one in which people get their wires crossed. Until we can see that contradictions are laughable, that the tragic and the comic go hand in hand, we will not be able to affirm the way our lives have been crossed and double-crossed.

Paul refers to the "scandal" of the cross, and in that word we see the comic dimension again. A scandal is cause for snickers and sly grins and all the other ways we indicate amusement when something happens which contradicts the prevailing order, the conventional scheme of things. The king has no clothing! The mighty have fallen! And that is what the cross is all about. Death is supposed to be the end. Resurrection is a scandal. When you think about it, it makes you laugh, that the powers of death, so arrogant and so certain of themselves, should be defeated on the cross! A scandal of the first order! The ultimate joke!

## LIBERATION

Recognition, resistance, acceptance, affirmation, and finally, the fifth station on this inward way of the cross: liberation. The finest fruit of the cross is liberation, not because freedom is an end in itself but because only as we become free can God use us. Free, I mean, from bondage to illusion, free from bondage to fear, free ultimately from the confusion of contradictions. On the cross we are liberated to live in truth, in love, in spontaneous responsiveness to the movement of the Spirit in our lives. Through the center of the cross we pass beyond contradiction into the wholeness of life in the Spirit.

The older word for liberation is "salvation," a difficult word to use these days because it has been so discredited by certain narrow-gauge versions of Christianity. But it is a word we need to reclaim, for its root meaning is "wholeness." To be saved is to be made whole, to be able to enter the unity that lies beyond all of life's contradictions.

Liberation will come only as we experience the cross in our lives; we must suffer the world's "no" in order to receive the divine "yes." Only by allowing life's contradictions to pull us open to the Spirit will we be able to live beyond the dualities that frighten us, the dualities of yes and no, day and night, right and wrong. Life on the way of the cross is, finally, a life of liberty in the Spirit, a life of salvation or wholeness in which contradictions are transcended. I have always liked the way John Middleton Murry spoke of such a life, ''For the good man to realize that it is better to be whole than to be good is to enter on a strait and narrow path compared to which his previous rectitude was flowery license.'' The liberation of the cross frees us not for indulgence and ease, but for the discipline of serving truth without fearing the contradictions.

To be saved, to be made whole, is to realize that we are in the contradictions, that the contradictions are in us, and that all of it is held together by a ''hidden wholeness.'' It is to be able to be anywhere with anyone, in freedom and in love. To be whole is to know one's relatedness to all of life, to the dark and the light, the evil and the good, the strange and the familiar. It is to walk freely across the earth knowing that God is with us whether we climb to the heavens or descend into hell. The liberation of the cross is knowing that there is no contradiction which God cannot overcome.

For those of us who are Christian, it is especially important to understand that the cross liberates us from narrow and confining versions of Christian faith itself. For the cross is not about one faith tradition, but about the power of God. Thomas Merton, Catholic Christian and Trappist monk, once put this in words which have always seemed quite remarkable to me:

> The Cross is the sign of contradiction—destroying the seriousness of the Law, of the Empire, of the armies. . . . But the magicians keep turning the cross to their own purposes. Yes, it is for them too a sign of contradiction: the awful blasphemy of the religious magician who makes the cross contradict mercy! This is of course the ultimate temptation of Christianity! To say that Christ has locked all the doors, has given one answer, settled everything and departed, leaving all life enclosed in the frightful consistency of a system outside of which there is seriousness and damnation, inside of which there is the intolerable flippancy of the saved—while nowhere is there any place left for the mystery of the freedom of divine mercy which alone is truly serious, and worthy of being taken seriously.[1]

Liberation is frightening; radical freedom scares us. That is why Erich Fromm was able to write about "the escape from freedom" as a characteristic of our time. Now Merton identifies the escape from freedom which has imprisoned too many Christian hearts—this tendency to draw tight the boundaries of salvation, to create a system of beliefs and practices which denies the radical freedom of God's mercy to move where it will, within the church and without. The cross finally contradicts any system of beliefs which tries to capture the cross. The movement of Christ in our lives, our sharing of his cross, liberates us from fear of freedom into freedom from fear. Only then are we fully available to one another, fully available to God.

1. Thomas Merton, "To Each His Darkness," in *Raids on the Unspeakable* (NY: New Directions, 1966).

# 3

## Paradoxes of Community
### (co-authored with Sally Palmer)

We had talked about community for years. How to create some "sense of community" where we lived? Whether to join an existing community—and which one? And what about the possibility of starting one with some of our friends? The longer we talked, the more barriers arose between us and any new way of life. Our family got larger, we all grew older, and as our needs increased our options narrowed. But the talk contained its own pressure, and by February of 1974 we knew it was time to put up or shut up. Our fantasies had become sources of frustration, not energy, and an honest look at ourselves revealed that we were beginning to protect life rather than live it.

The need for community came from our feelings of isolation and fragmentation both at work and at home. Sally's concerns revolved around the difficulties of raising three children in suburban seclusion, and of forming purposeful relations with other adults amidst the logistical chaos of a five-member family. Parker's needs involved the lack of community in academic life and the larger question of political community in America. Together we felt a need for community to simplify and integrate the disparate pieces of our lives.

Something had to give! So at the end of that dismal February, the five of us boarded a train and set off for Koinonia Partners in Americus, Georgia—a community we had read about for many years. Our calendar time there was only a week, but it was *kairos* time. The simple fact of seeing good people living in community, in faithful partnership with the victims of oppression, gave us new hope and direction. Someone down there spoke words we knew were true but had lacked the courage to say to ourselves: "You don't think your way into a new kind of living: you live your way into a new kind of thinking."

We returned to Washington committed to spend at least the next year in community, and took the first step with considerable trepidation: a leave of absence from Parker's job at the university. The prospect of twelve months without paychecks was not comforting, but we knew that nothing would happen as long as we remained comfortable.

Then began the search for a place. Koinonia Partners was a possibility, and so too was another Koinonia near Baltimore. We had read about the Bruderhof and corresponded with them. We visited Lindisfarne and Pendle Hill and got in touch with several other groups by phone and letter. These are quite different places, but they have this much in common: At each of them, a group of people is trying to live together and touch the world with some sort of religious understanding.

We finally chose Pendle Hill, a Quaker living-learning community near Philadelphia. Here we share a daily life of worship, study, physical work, common meals and recreation with some 60 people. Their ages range from one to seventy-one. About half, or fewer, are Quakers, and among the others many of the world's religions are represented. Pendle Hill is not a "pure" community; it is also an institution (an adult study center) with a staff, a board of managers, and a 50-year history. But here we have experienced one of the many versions in which community presents itself, and the experience has been compelling.

If it is true that one lives one's way into a new kind of thinking, it follows that one's ideas about a thing should change with experience. So it has been with our conception of community. We came to community with certain expectations; we came seeking certain qualities of life. We have found much of what we sought, but we have also found things we neither sought nor thought we wanted. In fact, it sometimes seems that for each thing we sought, we have found not only that thing but also its opposite!

We came seeking a fuller fellowship with others than we had experienced in the suburbs. We found it, but we also discovered a new need for solitude. We came seeking extended family for ourselves and our children. We found it, but we also discovered the need to draw our own family's boundaries more firmly around us. We came seeking to escape certain forces in the world. We have done so, but we have also found ourselves more deeply engaged with the world than ever before.

At first, these polarities were confusing and even demoralizing. We did not understand what was happening to us, why life in community so often pulled us between contradictions or impaled us on the horns of dilemmas. But the longer we live in community, the more we realize that these pairs are not contradictions or dilemmas at all. Instead, they have the character of paradox: both poles are true. When either extreme is taken alone the reality of human need is distorted. Only when the poles are held in creative tension with each other is the fullness of that need adequately expressed.

Take, for example, our wish for a richer group life. In the suburbs we were constantly pulled toward privatism. In fact, it sometimes seems to us that privacy is the major product which the affluent buy with their wealth. Expensive single-family houses full of mechanical aids, hired household services, costly cars and elaborate vacation getaways, all serve to keep us away from one another and to destroy any appearance of interdependence.

But independence is an unnatural condition for the human species, so beneath the apparent luxury of privatism lies a vast cavern of loneliness. We wanted readier access to other people. We wanted to be with them in a variety of settings—work, play, worship—not just on party nights. And we wanted more dependence, of us on others and others on us.

We found such relationships in this community, and we celebrate the way in which they have opened and enlarged our lives. But (and here beginneth the paradox) we have also discovered that in community loneliness can be intensified. When we feel lonely, it is much more difficult to be in a community where all around we can see friendships in which we do not share, than to be in a suburb where we can assume that everyone else is lonely too! That is, when the people here seem to be a community to each other but only a crowd to us, then our loneliness is more piercing than ever.

And now the paradox deepens. For in dealing with our own loneliness we have begun to understand the riches of solitude. Solitude is different from loneliness. Loneliness is a yearning for others which denies the fact that we are, humanly, alone to ourselves. Loneliness is often a refusal to face ourselves; it is rooted in the need to have the faces and voices of others fill up the emptiness we fear within. In solitude we face that condition directly, and we have found that our inward space can be full of light and silence and perhaps the experience of God—not an empty void. From solitude we emerge to create true community with others. But this is a community of persons who know themselves, not that colony of psychic parasites which sometimes passes for community.

So here is one paradox of community as we have experienced it: the need for group life and the need for solitude, each creating and deepening the other.

Another paradox involves our life as a family. We came to Pendle Hill hoping to broaden and extend our family boundaries. We wanted our children to know adults other than teachers and parents. And, as parents, we wanted the support of a larger group in bearing the burdens which weigh so heavily on the nuclear family.

All of that has happened, and more. Our 10-year-old son can often be found in the kitchen helping one of the young men here bake bread or peel vegetables. When we could not comfort our 7-year-old during his agonies as "the new boy at school," a 70-year-old woman gave him milk and cookies and autoharp lessons every day after school. Yesterday, our first-grade daughter took a blind woman from the community to school with her, escorting her through the morning's activities completely relaxed about her friend's "otherness."

For us, it has been important simply to see, up close, that our family's problems are not unique and to share solutions (and failures!) with other parents. We have also found that relations within the family are quickened and freshened by the view we get of one another through the eyes of others in the community. And in community we find that bad family patterns are more easily altered: if a morning squabble occurs, it is less likely to drag on through the day when we will soon be talking at breakfast with someone outside the vicious circle!

But here is the paradox. In our quest for an extended family of sorts, we have found the need to draw new boundaries around our nuclear family, to identify ourselves more clearly as a group within a group. The richness of association which community provides can also be experienced as a dispersion, a scattering of energies and attentions. We have found it vital to set aside family time and space, to become more conscious of family values, lest we begin to feel that we belong to everyone and thus to no one.

Our movement back toward family boundaries may have been motivated at first by fear of loss, but it has become a real affirmation of life together. Because of the community, we are now more aware of what it means to be a family. Community, with its tendency to diffuse family identity, has caused us to reflect more on the value of family life than we ever did when we were a group unto ourselves. And knowing we have a home within a home has freed us to participate even more fully in the larger group's life.

So, another paradox: the need to extend our family and the need to draw it in, each creating and deepening the other.

A third paradox begins with the fact that we came to community in part to escape certain forces in "the world." And, to some extent, we have succeeded. The pace here is more sane, the scale of things more human, our relations with others less anxious and competitive, and the pieces of our lives more integrated than before.

But "the world" is very much with us in community. If we have escaped some things, we have also had to engage ourselves and others at a depth to which we are not totally accustomed. Sometimes it is simply because others are impinging on our rights, or we on theirs, and in community there is no way to ignore those transgressions. Sometimes it is because community can be a psychic pressure cooker, forcing problems to the surface where they must be dealt with. If experiences like these are part of what we mean by "the world," then we have not escaped it here. On the contrary, we have been compelled to engage it more deeply.

But "the world" is more than individuals, their psyches and their relationships. It is also structures, powers and principalities, the events of history. It is people dying of starvation in Africa and of war in Southeast Asia. And though we continue to weep over our guilt for that world and our impotence in it, the deepening paradox of community is that we are beginning to feel more engaged with that world, too.

For one thing, community itself seems to be a witness worth making in a society gone mad with competitive individualism. Perhaps the recovery of our national political health will depend in part on the emergence of more small communities; numerous political theories suggest as much. For another thing, the community of which we are part is a community of conscience. More than that, it is a community which tries to listen for God's voice. We have come to feel that God has called us to community if for no other reason than to give us more ears with which to hear the Word. And, too, community makes it more possible to take those concrete actions which respond to God's claim on our lives. Simple living, for example, is facilitated by community; not only can we share resources, but we can encourage one another in a commitment to consume less. And community offers more support, psychic and otherwise, for the kind of risky action which our times seem to demand.

And so, another paradox of community: in seeking to escape certain forces in the world, we find ourselves more deeply engaged with the condition of our brothers and sisters.

We have not been well prepared to understand our lives in terms of paradox. Instead, we have been taught to see and think in dualisms: individual vs. group, self vs. others, contemplative vs. active, success vs. failure. But the deeper truths of our lives seem to need paradox for full expression. Both poles are true, and we live most creatively when we live between them in tension.

Perhaps even more can be said. Perhaps in the synthesis of those apparent opposites we get closer to truth. Perhaps in living beyond those dualisms we discover a truth which lies beyond mind's reach. In his book *Christian Zen,* William Johnston has written: ". . . it could be argued that Christianity is one tremendous koan that makes the mind boggle and gasp in astonishment; and faith is the breakthrough into that deep realm of the soul which accepts paradox . . . with humility."

Somehow, it seems right to us that community is the context in which we have begun to appreciate paradox. Always, in our mind's eye, we have seen community as a circle—and the circle is an image in which the apparent oppositions of life touch, meet, and flow continuously into one another. In that circle we are beginning to get a glimpse of the unity which may lie behind the apparent contradictions of experience.

We plan to stay on at Pendle Hill—probably three more years, possibly longer. For the time being, community is the context in which we want to live our lives. That could change, and radically: the ultimate paradox may be that an experience in community is incomplete without a season in the hermitage! If that happens, perhaps our understanding of paradox will have deepened enough to sustain us. The aim would be to see life steady and see it whole whether one is in the circle or out.

# 4

## A Place Called Community

---

We expect a theophany of which we know nothing but the place, and the place is called community.

—Martin Buber

### INTRODUCTION

Surely Buber's words are prophetic. God comes to us in the midst of human need, and the most pressing needs of our time demand community in response.

How can I participate in a fairer distribution of resources unless I live in a community which makes it possible to consume less? How can I learn accountability unless I live in a community where my acts and their consequences are visible to all? How can I learn to share power unless I live in a community where hierarchy is unnatural? How can I take the risks which right action demands unless I live in a community which gives support? How can I learn the sanctity of each life unless I live in a community where we can be persons, not roles, to one another?

In contrast to these hard questions the popular image of community is distressingly sentimental. We—especially white, middle-class folk—value community for the personal nurture it promises but ignore its challenges of political and economic justice. We speak of "life together" in romantic terms which bear little resemblance to the difficult discipline of a common life.

But the problems of our age will yield neither to personalism nor to romance. If the idea of community is to speak to our condition, we must change the terms of the discussion. So I write about community partly to correct the romantic fallacy. If we seek a dream community, reality will quickly defeat us, and the struggle for community cannot afford such losses.

I write, too, because the religious basis of community is so often ignored, and I believe that religion points not toward fantasy but toward ultimate reality. The idea of community is at the heart of every great religious tradition. The Hebrew Bible is primarily the narrative of a community making and breaking its covenant with God. The New Testament affirms that the capacity to join with others in a life of prayer and service is one test of receiving God's spirit. The Acts of the Apostles, for example, reports that the formation of a community of shared goods was among the firstfruits of Pentecost:

> All whose faith had drawn them together held everything in common: they would sell their property and possessions and make a general distribution as the need of each required (Acts 2:44-45).

And from the heart of my own spiritual experience I know that God is constantly moving within and among us, calling us back to that unity, that community, in which we were created. If we will respond to that call, we can make a critical witness to the possibility of a future both human and divine. In the pages that follow, I shall try to show how and why.


## QUEST FOR COMMUNITY

Much has been made about the quest for community in our day, but our rhetoric is not reflected in our actions. While we honor community with words, the history of the 20th century has been a determined movement away from life together.

For at least three generations Americans have been in

conscious flight from the communities of family and town. Both the extended family and the small town slowed our progress toward a goal we cherish more deeply than we cherish life together: the goal of economic mobility. The small town cannot contain a range of jobs wide enough or tall enough to permit us freedom of movement. And when we do get a chance to move onward and upward, the extended family holds us back.

So we have been drawn toward cities large and complicated enough to meet our economic desires, and toward families small and portable (and even disposable) enough to make mobility possible. Popular sociology portrays us as victims of these "movements" and "trends," as if the woes that accompany modernity had been forced upon us. But no. The destruction of intimate community has been at our own hands. It has corresponded to our own hierarchy of values. My point is not that large cities and small families are wrong; both clearly have their values. My point is that those values stand largely in tension with the value of total and intimate community. As much as we yearn for community, we yearn even more for the social and economic prizes individual mobility can bring.

We can take a first, crucial step away from romance about community by recognizing that it is a value in conflict with other values we hold—and in our decisions, community usually loses out. How many of us would pass up a job promotion which involved relocation in favor of deepening our local roots? How many of us would trade the anonymity of the city (no matter how lonely at times) for the cloying, gossipy, parochial place we imagine small-town America to be? We must begin by recognizing that our verbal homage to community is only one side of a deep ambivalence that runs through the American character—the other side of which is a celebration of unfettered individualism.

## THE RESURGENCE OF INDIVIDUALISM

In times past, this American ambivalence was anchored strongly on two sides, for both individualism and community seemed possible. The settlers of the American frontier had to possess both the strength of individuality and the capacity for community. They needed to stand alone and to stand together, and there seemed to be no contradiction between the two. But in our time, individualism has run amok. We remain ambivalent, but one anchor has been tugged loose, and we find ourselves drifting dangerously toward the rocks of autonomy and the isolated self because we can no longer be certain that community is available to us.

The breakdown of confidence in community has been explored by Philip Rieff in *The Triumph of the Therapeutic*. Rieff argues that community itself once prevented disintegration of the individual personality, for in community each self had its boundaries and its place. Absent were anxieties about whether one was needed, and where; the answers were woven into the very fabric of society. And in the event that a personality did crumble, community itself was the therapy. In community one could find the confining but comforting role which brought life back together.

But with the breakdown of the common life came growing personal disintegration and the need for a therapy which did not depend on community! So, Rieff points out, a new mode of therapy emerged (notably Freudian) aimed at creating individuals who could function without corporate support, persons who could get along without others. As Rieff notes, these are not only the goals of therapy, they are themes reinforced by the therapeutic process itself. For example, the "crisis of transference" is that point at which the patient must learn to become independent even of the therapist. And the sheer expense of therapy is a constant reminder to the patient that aid will not come freely from the community but must be purchased in the marketplace. Much of modern therapy is premised on the notion that community is no longer available and we had better learn to go it alone.

This theme pervades other areas of modern life. Education is a notable example. Historically, education and community were inseparable. The content of education reflected the community consensus, and at the same time helped the community evolve and perpetuate itself. Today education has become a training ground for competition, rooted in the assumption that community is gone and we must learn to stand on our own two feet. In fact, more than a training ground, education itself has become a competitive arena where winners and losers are determined even before the contest is scheduled to begin.

It is not only that isolated practices in the schools—like grading on the curve—are so obviously rooted in Social Darwinism. It is not only that when students get together to cooperate on their work, most schools call it "cheating"—so suspect are the communal virtues. Nor is it only that most of us, deep inside, feel that children who are trained to cooperate rather than compete are not well prepared for the "real world." Beneath these surface symptoms is a fundamental fact: our schools perform an economic function more than an educational one; they exist not so much to teach and learn as to play a role in the distribution of scarce goods and resources. Their function, that is, no longer involves reflecting and renewing the community but providing the means by which society can decide who gets what, and how much of it.

The same premise—that community is gone and we must learn to stand alone—can be found in much that passes for the "new spirituality" these days. For in religious life, too, community has disappointed and failed us. Many who understand themselves as religious, or who are open to religious experience, cannot tolerate the church in any of its forms. So the new religions, with their emphasis on the solitary journey of the inward-seeking self, have found many followers.

At their worst, these new religions have made the self not only the vehicle but also the object of the religious quest. In these quarters, psychology is praised for having cut through centuries of theological obfuscation and God is found to be identical with the Self. Not that the self is made in God's image, or that in every self can be found that of God. No, in this new faith God and Self are taken to be one and the same. Lost is the confrontation between God and self, as they become comfortably absorbed into one another. And lost is the sense that the self is defined by participation in communities of covenant. It is no accident that contemporary religious jargon so frequently refers to "getting in touch with one's self." Those words replace what another age meant by "seeking the face of God," because we have lost confidence that anything beyond the self exists or can be trusted.

## THE RISK OF SEEKING COMMUNITY

The assumption that community is increasingly hard to find is well founded. It *is* difficult to find or create relationships of duration and reliability in our kind of world. But such realism quickly becomes pernicious: every time we act on that assumption, every time we gird ourselves to go it alone, we create more of the same reality. The assumption that community cannot be counted upon is a self-fulfilling prophecy, for as we act on it we become men and women who do not call others to accountability and cannot be counted on ourselves. "Crackpot realism" is what C. Wright Mills would have called it, for its eventual outcome can only be the war of all against all. We need to find the courage to assert and act upon the hope, however naive, that community can be found, because only by acting "as if" can we create a future fit for human habitation.

We will find that courage only as we come to a new understanding of what it means to seek health for our personal lives. We live in a time of extreme self-consciousness, a time of self-doubt, self-examination, self-help. We seem aware of every inner perturbation, as if we had been born with psychic seismographs capable of measuring each movement along our personal fault lines. Ours is a time in which health is supposed to come by focussing on ourselves and by seeking the resources for self-renewal.

But we've got it all backwards! For self-health is one of those strange things in human life which eludes those who aim directly at it, but comes to those who aim elsewhere. It was best said in the words of Jesus: "He who finds his life will lose it, and he who loses his life for my sake will find it." So we must learn, in this twisted age, that the ultimate therapy is to identify our own pain with the pain of others, and then band together to resist the conditions that create our common malady.

The ultimate therapy is to translate our private problems into corporate issues. In doing so we will discover that some of our private problems are too trivial to be dignified with public status, and they will fall away. But others, we will discover, are not private at all—they are common to our time. And as we learn to see our own plight in the lives of our sisters and brothers we will begin to find health. Therapy involves identifying and building communities of concern. Only so can we heal ourselves.

All this inverts our conventional wisdom. Most of us fear community because we think it will call us away from ourselves. We are afraid that in community our sense of self will be overpowered by the identity of the group. We pit individuality and community against one another, as if a choice had to be made, and increasingly we choose the former.

But what a curious conception of self we have! We have forgotten that the self is a moving intersection of many other selves. We are formed by the lives which intersect ours. The larger and richer our community, the larger and richer is the content of the self. There is no individuality without community; thus, the surprising finding that an affluent suburb with all its options, but without community, may nurture individuality less than a provincial village with few choices but a rich community life.

So the way to self, and to self-health, is the way of community. We have lost a true sense of self in our time because we have lost community. But lost things can be found. Community can be rebuilt as more men and women find within themselves the need and the willingness to risk community. And the risk is only apparent. From where we are, it appears that the chances for community are slim. And once in community, the pain of losing one's fantasies is fierce. But on the other side of all that there is no risk at all, only the confidence that life was meant to be lived together.

## POLITICS OF COMMUNITY

If the ultimate therapy is to build community then building community is the ultimate politics. Community is a place where therapy and politics meet, for here the health of the individual and the health of the group may be seen for the reciprocal realities that they are.

The link between therapy and politics is clear in the problem of loneliness, that painful fact of so many modern lives which community is supposed to cure. But loneliness is not just a personal problem. It has political causes and consequences. We are lonely because a mass society keeps us from engaging one another on matters of common destiny. And loneliness makes us prey to a thousand varieties of political manipulation. Our loneliness renders us not only pathetic but politically dangerous. If we could understand that fact we might create communities which contribute to political and personal health by more fairly distributing the power of decision over our personal and corporate destinies.

Political scientists have long known that community in all its forms plays a key role in the distribution of power. Families, neighborhoods, work teams, churches, and other voluntary associations stand between the lone individual and the power of the central state. They provide the person with a human buffer zone so that he or she does not stand alone against the state's demands. They amplify the individual's small voice so it can be heard by a state which turns deaf when it does not want to listen. In such communities we gain skill at negotiating our interest with the interests of the group. If these communities decline in number or in quality the condition known as "mass society" sets in. Mass society is characterized not simply by size, but by the fact that individuals in it do not have organic relations with one another, only a common membership in the nation-state. In mass society the person stands alone against the state, without a network of communal associations to protect personal meaning, to enlarge personal power, or to teach the habits of democracy.

The loneliness of mass men and women is a measure of their political impotence, and given that impotence—that inability to act together—the step from mass society to totalitarianism is short indeed. In a totalitarian society the state exercises careful control over the number and content of intermediary communities so they will not empower individuals to resist the state. In a democracy, as community begins to wither, the conditions are ripe for totalitarianism to take root.

We sadly mistake the task of politics if we focus all our efforts on petitioning or pressuring the institutions of government toward certain ends. The functioning of democratic institutions depends on the existence of a community, a community to which government is accountable, a community which gives people the power to make claims on those who govern. More than that, community is the context in which people come to understand their inter-relatedness. Without such understanding people will have no interest in government at all, except as it impinges directly on their self-interest. So community is a precondition of a democratic politics, and the building of community is an essential pre-political task.

But the American condition seems to be one of deepening privatism. Affluence (or the desire to maintain the image of it) draws us into life-styles designed to protect us from sight and sound of one another. Goods and services which we might share, or even provide for one another, become individual consumer items, thus weakening the fabric of community. We are more anxious to protect our roles as consumers than to develop our roles as citizens, more desirous of being able to buy our autonomy than letting our interdependence show.

In truth, of course, we are interdependent, despite our expensive efforts to construct a facade of autonomy. As the world economic crisis deepens, we will continue to learn just how interdependent we are. We will learn how self-defeating is the war of all against all, with each trying to get a more-than-fair share of the pie.

We have already had intimations of how such an awareness might move us back toward community. At the height of the recent "fuel shortage" people quickly learned to share automobile transportation with their neighbors.

But that crisis passed, and the sharing passed with it. As such crises multiply, there will probably be an interim period in which old habits of competition and acquisitiveness will assert themselves with renewed vigor as people struggle to ward off the dawning knowledge that things will never be the same. It will be some time before the worldwide pressure to share becomes so great as to make community the only sensible option. Until then, we can expect more and more of the economic individualism that possesses us now.

So those who cultivate the instincts of community in themselves, and labor to build its external forms, are engaged in a task whose success is critical. The politics and economics of community are fundamental, and until we understand their full implications our image of community will continue to be pleasantly irrelevant. Community means more than the comfort of souls. It means, and has always meant, the survival of species.


## TRUE COMMUNITY OR FALSE?

But the longer we sing the praises of community, the more we court another romantic fallacy: that to say "community" is to say "good." Not so. Selma, Cicero, South Boston: these were all communities, but false ones. As we learn the difference between true community and false we will move even farther from sentimentality about the common life.

In fact, the most notable example of false community is the totalitarian society to which the decline of true community leads. In the midst of mass loneliness people yearn to identify with something larger than themselves, something which will redeem their lives from insignificance. They yearn, that is, for community, for that network of human associations which enlarges the individual's life. This hunger runs so deep that even the appearance of community will feed it, and totalitarianism always presents itself as a communal feast for the masses. What was Nazi Germany except a demonic form of community life? What is any brand of nationalism or racism except the idea of community run amok?

The differences between true community and false could be listed at length. For instance, false communities tend to be manipulated by the state, while true community is independent of governmental power. That is, in true communities people will be free to relate to one another in ways that are contrary to established power, while in false communities that power protects itself by setting strict limits on acceptable association.

In false communities the group is always superior to the individual, while in true communities both individual and group have a claim on truth. The critique of individualism in the preceding pages was not intended to degrade the concrete individual, but to insist that the individual needs to be checked and balanced by the group. The converse is also true. The group needs to be checked and balanced by the individual's voice, for majorities do not mean truth. In false communities the concrete individual is swallowed up in abstractions about "blood, soil, and race." True communities are built upon the person perceived, not abstractions about persons.

False communities tend to be homogenous, exclusive, and divisive, while true communities strive to unite persons across socially fixed lines. We should be suspicious of any "community" which forms too quickly, too easily, for it is likely to depend on social categories which make not for community but for commonality. And commonality does not nurture the human growth and expansiveness which true community provides.

But beyond all these sociological distinctions between true community and false, there is a theological way of expressing the differences which brings us to the heart of the matter. False communities are idolatrous. They take some finite attribute like race, creed, political ideology, or even manners, and elevate it to ultimacy. They seek security by trying to make timeless that which is temporal; by pretending that which is shaky is firm; by worshiping that which should be viewed critically. They confuse their own power with the power of God and tragically try to use that power to decide questions of life and death. False communities are ultimately demonic, which is not to say that true communities are divine, for both retain their human character. But true communities will take the form of covenant. They will experience both God's mercy and God's judgment in their lives.

These categories are not fixed, for a false community can turn true, and a true community can turn false. Indeed, one danger in any true form of community life is self-confidence and pride which turn toward idolatry and falseness. A true community is a self-critical community always ready to deflate its pretensions before they balloon up to deity size. A true community must be ready to criticize its current conception of whatever it holds most dear, for at that point the greatest danger of idolatry occurs.

All of this reminds us again that community is finally a religious phenomenon. There is nothing capable of binding together willful, broken human selves except some transcendent power. But not all such power is creative or even benign. What that power is, and what it demands of those who rely upon it—these are factors that determine the quality of a community's life.

## SOME MYTHS ABOUT COMMUNITY

Any further effort to define true community and its sources will require the destruction of several romantic myths, myths which have replaced the reality of community in contemporary thought.

There is first the myth that community is a creature comfort which can be added to a life full of other luxuries. For the affluent, community has become another consumer item. You can buy it in weekend chunks at human potential centers, or you and your friends can have it by purchasing a piece of country property.

But, in truth, community is another one of those strange things (like self-health) which eludes us if we aim directly at it. Instead, community comes as a by-product of commitment and struggle. It comes when we step forward to right some wrong, to heal some hurt, to give some service. Then we discover each other as allies in resisting the diminishments of life. It is no accident that the most impressive sense of community is found among people in the midst of such joyful travail: among blacks, among women, among all who have said no to tyranny with the yes of their lives.

Of all the myths of community, this one will be the hardest to overcome. For the world teaches us to go after what we want—directly, aggressively, single-mindedly. But community, approached that way, stays constantly beyond our reach. We cannot have it just because we want it—precisely because the foundation of community itself goes beyond selfishness into life for others. Only as our beliefs and acts link us to the invisible community of humankind will the forms of visible community grow up around us.

Another myth tells us that community equals utopia, that in easy access to one another supportive relationships will result and we will find ourselves brothers and sisters again. But community always means the collision of egos.

It is less like utopia than like a crucible or a refiner's fire. In this process God wants us to learn something about ourselves, our limits, our need for others. In this process there is the pain of not getting our way, but the promise of finding the Way.

Dietrich Bonhoeffer knew this fact about community well:

> Innumerable times a whole Christian community has broken down because it had sprung from a dream wish. . . . God's grace speedily shatters such dreams. Just as surely as God desires to lead us to a knowledge of genuine Christian fellowship, so surely must we be overwhelmed by a great disillusionment with others, with Christians in general, and, if we are fortunate, with ourselves . . . God is not a God of the emotions but the God of truth . . . He who loves his dream of a community more than the Christian community itself becomes a destroyer of the latter, even though his personal intentions may be ever so honest and earnest and sacrificial. (*Life Together,* pp. 26-27)

Bonhoeffer is right about the destructive potential of being in love with one's dream of community, and this is why the utopian myth must be denied. For those who come into community with only that dream will soon leave, hurt, resentful, and probably lost to the cause of community-building. But those who can survive the failure of their dream and the abrasion of their egos will find that the reality of community is richer and more supportive than fantasy can ever be. For in community one learns that self is not an adequate measure of reality; that we can begin to know the fullness of truth only through multiple visions.

The great danger in our utopian dreams of community is that they lead us to want association with people just like ourselves. Here we confront the third myth of community—that it will be an extension and expansion of our own egos, a confirmation of our own partial view of reality. I have often heard it argued that in a real community, the group would have absolute power to select new members and thus control the degree of dissonance within.

But I think not. In a true community we will not choose our companions, for our choices are so often limited by self-serving motives. Instead, our companions will be given to us by grace. Often they will be persons who will upset our settled view of self and world. In fact, we might define true community as that place where the person you least want to live with always lives!

If we live this way we can avoid the trap that Richard Sennett has called "the purified community." Here, as in the typical suburb, one is surrounded by likeness to the extent that challenge is unlikely and growth is impossible. In true community there will be enough diversity and conflict to shake loose our need to make the world in our own image. True community will teach us the meaning of the prayer, "Thy will, not mine, be done."

In exploring and exploding each of these myths we are reminded again that true community is a spiritual reality which lies beyond social and psychological principles. If Martin Buber was right that in turning to each other we turn to God, then community is a context for conversion (literally, "a turning"). And what community can convert us to lies on several levels. Community reminds us that we are called to love, for community is a product of love in action and not of simple self-interest. Community can break our egos open to the experience of a God who cannot be contained by our conceptions. Community will teach us that our grip on truth is fragile and incomplete, that we need many ears to hear the fullness of God's word for our lives. And the disappointments of community life can be transformed by our discovery that the only dependable power for life lies beyond all human structures and relationships.

In this religious grounding lies the only real hedge against the risk of disappointment in seeking community.

That risk can be borne only if it is not community one seeks, but truth, light, God. Do not commit yourself to community, but commit yourself to the God who stands beyond all human constructions. In that commitment you will find yourself drawn into community. And in that commitment the difficult lessons of community can be borne and transformed into a larger and truer life.

## FORMS OF LIFE TOGETHER

Clearly community is a process. But it is also a place. When Buber says, "We expect a theophany of which we know nothing but the place, and the place is called community," he suggests how process and place are intertwined. For theophany, the meeting with the living God is obviously dynamic and full of movement. But for Christians and Jews that meeting always happens in the concrete places of this world. It is important to retain that sense of place lest community become one of those diffuse and disembodied words which excite our imaginations but never confront us with daily reality.

As we consider the forms of community life, we run into the cultural arrogance of the recent communal movement and its assumption that the small, intentional community, withdrawn from the larger society, is the only worthy form of the common life. Clearly the emergence of such communes is important to us. They do provide models, and they serve as schools for less intensive forms of life together. But they are out of reach for many people. We need to help one another build community where we are, rather than encouraging dreams which turn to despair over a community which for many of us will never be. We need to foster the diverse forms of community which are needed if an urban, technological society is to recover its human roots.

For some of us, the community to build is the family, that ancient unit of common life which has been much maligned in modern thought. If our efforts are to be honest, however, we must weigh the chances of family life against the economic aspirations which have contributed to the family's failure. For decades the family has been torn apart by our own desires for personal advancement. We have weakened and even destroyed the family by opting for personal mobility and economic success. We will rebuild community in the family only if the lure of achievement can take second place to the cultivation of relations between the generations.

The importance of doing so seems clear and urgent. For many people, the family is the place where the difficulty, even the impossibility, of community is first sensed. If one grows up in a family where attempts at intimacy are frustrated, where trust does not exist and support cannot be found, one becomes an adult fearful of further rejection, an adult who will not risk community again.

If it seems idealistic to suppose that many people will place community of any sort ahead of financial gain, consider that the prospect of shrinking world resources may force us to do just that. Many of us, and our children, will no longer be able to ride up the economic escalator. Unable to move on, we may learn to pay attention to what is around us. And a levelling economy will compel us to share more fully than we do now—a sharing which means some form of extended family.

The impact of economic trends on family life is nowhere more evident than in the growing aspirations of women for a full and rightful share of both work and compensation. The mothering force that held the family together in previous generations was based partly on the exclusion of women from the ranks of paid workers. As women lay claim to their economic rights, it becomes clear that men must more fully share the tasks of family nurture if the family is to be a model of community life.

That it can be a model of great power seems clear. For example, many of us find it impossible to think about a real community of goods, in which each person contributes resources according to ability and draws out resources according to need. We cannot imagine a community in which we would contribute to the common pot and watch others, regardless of their ability to contribute, take out what they need. Yet those of us who come from strong families do precisely that within the family circle. We have no question that a child or a spouse who earns no money has full claim on our resources for educational needs, medical aid, and so forth. Perhaps we can move toward larger expressions of community by asking how to enlarge our sense of who belongs to the family.

For others among us, the community to build is in our neighborhoods—which tend to be held together more by mortgages and zoning laws than by love of neighbor. And again, most of us want it that way. We want to protect some private space in our busy lives, to stay loose of entanglements with those who live next door, to be free to move without the pain of breaking bonds when job advancement calls us elsewhere.

The breakdown of neighborhoods is directly related to the political health of the larger society. For without local forms of community it is impossible for people to have true community on a national scale. In political terms, local community is not just a nicety. Instead, it is the source of citizenship, the wellspring of feelings of relatedness, responsibility, and efficacy. The sense of impotence that so many feel today is directly related to the failure of local community; one has no hope of influencing a nation if one does not have a local community to help govern.

In our mobile, metropolitan life, it takes some external force to make a neighborhood become aware of itself as a community. In recent years that force has been the simple fact of change in the racial and economic composition of an area. For the most part, of course, such change has been viewed negatively and defensively. It has caused false community to form, a community which fearfully excludes those who are somehow different.

But more positive outcomes are possible. For several years, in suburban Washington, D.C., there was a project aimed at helping white middle-class people cope with community change. The core of that project was a series of "living room seminars" which brought together ten or fifteen neighbors in an eight-week curriculum designed to help them identify and overcome the sources of their resistance to change.

The people in these seminars, once they got past their myths and stereotypes, did not want to run from change but wanted to meet it and learn from it. Their inability to do so resulted largely from their lack of community. The feeling that they stood alone in the confusions of change made them fearful and brittle. Having identified this need in themselves, members of the seminars set out to build community in small but concrete ways. One group, for example, developed a "Neighborhood Resource Catalog," listing the interests and skills that residents would be willing to share with one another. These exchanges themselves were community-builders, and so also was the simple act of going door to door asking neighbors what they would like to list in the catalog. We need excuses, it seems, to meet our neighbors. But when we do, face to face, community begins to happen, and fear of "those people" begins to recede. In small but significant ways, projects such as these helped neighbors become neighbors.

Together, people are able to replace the images of fear with the human face of community.

Others among us may be called to build community in the places where we go to school and work. These have become the major areas of hierarchy and competition for many Americans. In them we are pitted against one another so that something called "higher performance" may be achieved. But when we destroy the community of work we get unethical products and degrading service. When we destroy the community of scholars, dehumanized teaching and learning are the result. We will build community in these places only if we see that performance at the expense of community is no achievement at all.

Most of us should be deeply challenged by the idea that cooperation rather than competition is the source of genuinely creative work, for we have been programmed to exert the greatest effort in competitive situations where our instinct to win is exploited. Most of us, deep down, believe that education which does not rank individuals in relation to each other is simply not sufficiently rigorous. We are dubious of the benign assumptions about human motivation which lie behind group projects where everyone is supposed to "win," and no one need "lose."

There is some evidence, however, that the group really is more intelligent and perceptive than any single member of it. I think, for example, of those simulation games which pose a problem for individuals to solve on their own and then allow a period of time for those individuals to share and correct each other's solution. Almost always the group solution is nearer to the right answer than is the solution of any individual in the group. Often the difference is dramatic. If evidence such as this were taken seriously, the competitive individualism of both school and work might begin to be transformed. And with it, one suspects, would come not only a higher level of personal satisfaction, but also of problem-solving and creativity.

## THE CHURCHES AND COMMUNITY

It seems ironic to suggest that some of us may be called to build community in our churches, for if we have any model of true community it is the church as it was meant to be. But the church is a human reality as well as divine, and clearly it has failed to be the kind of community God (and some of us) had in mind.

And yet the church, more than any other major institution in our society, still contains the potential for true community life. The symbols of community are there. The tradition of community stands behind us. And sometimes the leadership for community is present as well.

Most important, the church contains a more typical cross section of people than any institution around, a human diversity which is held together (in theory) by commitment to a truth which transcends our differences. In practice, the church often tries to suppress the diversity it contains, and when it fails fragmentation is the result. But the church might yet learn to deal with its secondary differences in the context of its ultimate unity. If that were to happen, the church would be the most compelling model of community on the American scene.

The core of the Christian tradition is a way of inward seeking which leads to outward acts of integrity and service, acts of love. Christians are most in the Spirit when they stand at the crossing point of the inward and the outward life. And at that intersection, community is found. Community is a place where the connections felt in our hearts make themselves known in the bonds between people, and where the tuggings and pullings of those bonds keep opening up our hearts.

The church can make its greatest contribution to community by persisting in its worship—by persisting, I mean in the practice of the presence of God. Again, community is simply too difficult to be sustained by our social impulses. It can be sustained only as we return time and again to the spiritual experience of the unity of all life. To put it in the language of Quakers, community happens as that of God in you responds to that of God in me. And the affirmation that there is that of God in every person must mean more than "I'm OK, you're OK." It must mean a constant renewal of our sense of sacredness in every life.

In many of our churches, we might do well to give more time for the sacrament of silence as we worship together. I am an orthodox, garden-variety Christian, and I need to hear the words of faith spoken and affirmed. But I also know that much of religious truth is simply inexpressible, that words can divide us while in the silence truth can bring us together. Whatever kinds of worshiping communities the world needs, it surely needs those that embrace our diversity within a truth that transcends creeds.

But in the silence, in religious mysticism, there are dangers as well. The mystical experience of unity which we find in meditation is not often manifest in the realm of human relations, and those who seek mystical unity may be tempted to scorn or flee the imperfections of outward life. Or we may be tempted to worship the silence itself, forgetting that contemplation is only a vehicle in which God may come to disrupt as well as comfort us. Both of these temptations are idolatries, and both of them stand in the way of community. If we forsake the problems of human relations for the sake of the silent life, then community will be impossible for us.

What we need is not simply the individual at prayer, seeking his or her own sacred space. We need a corporate practice which seeks a space in which we can all stand together. In worship we need to know that God wants to bring us together as a gathered people; that we must listen to each other, in the words and in the silences between them, testing our own truth against the truth received by others. We must trust that God will work a greater truth in all of us than can be worked in any one of us standing alone.

Here is where Christians can contribute to community by refusing to follow the religious individualism of our times. Behind many of the new spiritual movements lies the assumption that truth is totally subjective—one truth for you, another for me, and never mind the difference. But when we understand truth that way then the truth we are given will have no chance to transform society or ourselves. If we affirm community we must take the risk that our own version of truth will be enlarged, or even made uncouth, by the light given to others.

If true community is to flourish then the individual must flourish as well. So as the church seeks corporate truth, it must be ever mindful of the light which an individual can be given. In our corporate seeking, the individual must never be overpowered, never coerced into going along, never put in the position of an outvoted and embittered minority. Christians can contribute to community by walking the way that lies between religious authoritarianism and spiritual subjectivism. As the church tests for corporate truth, it must always respect the word of God in the single heart, a word which may be too radical for the group to hear.

The truth that Christians have been given has led them into some of the hard places of history, places where truth must speak to power. And in these places the living experience of community has been found. Mildred Binns Young has written of the communal life among the first generation of Quakers who brought suffering after suffering upon themselves simply by living out the light of Christ which dwelt within them. She speaks of the fact that under these "all but annihilating persecutions" Quakers "drew people to them as [they] never have since." Those Friends did not have to devise fancy schemes for keeping in touch with one another, for generating a community life. Instead, "their necessities kept them together"—such necessities as the need to care for Friends in prison, and for their stranded children; the need to share what few animals and tools were left after the tax collectors had confiscated most of them; the need to petition authorities for relief from injustice. "So," writes Mildred Young, "a Friends meeting, without any theories of communalism, had in effect something like it."

Theory can only provide clues. Community comes from faithful living. If Christians can lead such lives in the context of family and neighborhood, of school and workplace, and in the politics of our times, then we will contribute to the creation of a community both human and divine. There is no witness more urgent for our day.

# 5

## A World of Scarcity—A Gospel of Abundance

Scarcity and abundance are basic terms in the political and economic travail of our times. The world is split into "haves" and "have-nots," into those who have more than enough to eat and stay warm and those who lack even enough to survive. With predictions of dwindling natural resources, and with growing pessimism over technology's ability to bridge the gap, even we "haves" begin to know fear. And in our fear we consume and hoard even more, thus further imbalancing the scales of global justice.

These things are widely known. But perhaps it is not so commonly understood that scarcity and abundance are also basic terms in our spiritual lives. We have not said enough about the connection between our state of spiritual awareness and our ability to respond to these political and economic wrongs. To a considerable extent it is the quality of our contemplation which will dictate whether we find life pinched and cramped and fearful, or open, expansive, and free. If our inner life is an experience of scarcity and grasping, we will surely not live an outward witness to free sharing of earth's goods.

In this essay, I want to examine the world's scarcity and God's promise of abundance. I want to look at scarcity and abundance as aspects of the spiritual quest. And I want to suggest three ways in which we can help ourselves and each other move from the life-destroying habits of scarcity toward the life-affirming instincts of abundance: the ways of education, community and prayer.

## THE SCARCITY ASSUMPTION

More than we know, our lives are governed by rules—not the rules of civil society, but rules which flow from the assumptions we make about life. Each of us is filled with such assumptions, with beliefs about "how things are" and what we can expect. More than we know, our attitudes and behaviors are shaped by these beliefs, beliefs we hardly ever examine because we think they simply reflect reality. If we think life is a jungle, then that's the way life is likely to be for us—not because life really is a jungle but because the assumption leads us to act in ways that cause the jungle to grow up around us. The paranoid person eventually creates the very enemies that began only in his or her imagination. These prophecies come true not because they are inevitable, but because we bring them to life by acting *as if* they were true.

So it is with scarcity and abundance. Are the basic goods of life plentiful or in short supply? It depends. It depends on your assumptions. What do you assume those basic goods to be? If diamonds are vital to you, or if you absolutely must have mangoes, then scarcity becomes a problem. And what do you assume about the sources of supply? If all life's goods must be obtained through cash exchange with others, it will be hard to see the abundance that lies beyond dependence on the market.

Most people seem to assume that scarcity is a simple fact of life. How else can one explain the obsession with acquiring, consuming and hoarding which permeates our society? We live in constant fear of the future—the fear that money will run out, that food supplies will dwindle, that housing will be unavailable. And as we act on those fears, the assumption becomes reality! As we consume more than we need, as we hoard against the future, then stores do dwindle and prices do rise and there will be too little to go around.

The tragic victims of this self-fulfilling prophecy are, of course, the "have-nots" of the world who lack the capital to act out their economic fears. For them, scarcity is no assumption at all: It is a hard and cruel fact of life. But that fact is created by people who have a choice—the choice to assume scarcity and grab for all one can get, or the choice to assume abundance and live in such a way as to create and share it. For these people—for those of us who are affluent and educated—the matter of choosing assumptions is more than academic. Our souls and the lives of others hang in the balance.

## THE REALITY OF ABUNDANCE

As we look at nature, at what is simply and freely given to us in creation, we cannot help but be impressed with its abundance. Properly treated, nature seems capable of infinite self-replenishment. Seeds grow in fertile soil; animals multiply apace; the soil is recreated by the death of flora and fauna; the earth is fecund beyond imagination. And what nature does not supply ready-made, a humane technology is able to fabricate: amalgams and compounds and derivatives for meeting our every need. Set aside for a moment our misuse of the earth and the madness which has overtaken our technology, and simply contemplate the abundance of nature and human inventiveness, in its right order.

In the midst of such abundance, how can we explain the scarcity assumption? Surrounded by a grace which seems capable of meeting reasonable human needs, how did we end up with things in short supply?

One answer lies in our tendency to overvalue things according to the whims of the community and the culture. When we exaggerate the importance of something, when we hinge our happiness on our ability to own it, and when thousands of us are obsessed with the same thing at the same time, then that thing either becomes scarce or priced beyond reach.

Another answer lies in our habit of arbitrarily limiting the sources of supply. Vegetables can be grown almost anywhere there is black earth, but when we insist on putting much of that earth in lawns and other decorations, or under shopping centers and highways, we limit agriculture and make its issue scarce. It is not that nature has become less generous; it is rather that we have chosen to reject her gifts.

But what is truly remarkable about the human animal is not only that we take physical abundance and make it scarcity, but that we do the same with the infinite supply of goods of the Spirit! It is one thing to overvalue diamonds or undersupply tomatoes and find them scarce. It is quite another thing to treat love and affection and trust and regard as entities in short supply. And yet, how many of us do exactly that? How often, in our relationships, do we act as if the stores of love were limited, and if she gets too much of it there will be too little left for me? Is this not the basis of all human jealousies and envies, this instinct that there are not enough of these Spirit-goods to go around?

Or take a human good like pleasure or fun. Clearly, the ways of having fun are infinite, limited only by our imaginations. But how many people spend weekends and summers resenting that they lack the money to *really* have fun—or that all the money they spent failed to buy enough of the product? We have limited the supply of "fun," and have put the power to "produce" it in the hands of sports promoters, casino operators and travel agents. We have put ourselves in the position of anxious and impoverished consumers wanting to buy from the approved sources but with never enough cash or enough satisfaction to come out ahead. We have made that which is obviously abundant into that which is scarce.

Or take another intangible—education. Clearly, education is a vast adventure of the human spirit, possible in any place, under any circumstance, with any material one can imagine. What are the limits on learning or teaching? There are none. Why, then, have we put boundaries around education, called the result "schools," and made schooling an object of bitter competition? Why have we taken that which is limitless in nature and made it scarce, creating a situation in which people's self-esteem, and often the course of their lives, is determined by the fact that some get more and some get less?

## THE DYNAMICS OF SCARCITY

Why, indeed? The more one presses that question the more puzzling it becomes. Once we recognize how much of this scarcity we impose upon ourselves, and once we recognize how that brings us little else but grief, the more one has to wonder why we willfully choose the lesser portion. Why do we choose self-defeat?

It is too easy (for those of us who are affluent and educated) to blame it on the politics and economics of greed. Clearly such greed is at work. If you can convince people that they need something, and/or limit and control its supply, then you have either power or wealth, and the one leads to the other. So there is self-interest, for some, in creating scarcities where none exist, and self-interest is ample explanation for any human behavior.

But the self-interest of some does not explain why the rest of us succumb to their definitions of scarcity. Just because someone wants to gain power and wealth by trying to promote an illusion of scarcity, why should we accept the illusion? Why do most of us let the kings of scarcity

walk down the streets naked without ever shouting out
"The king has no clothing!"?

The answer to that question probes to the deepest level
of our spiritual condition. For our devotion to the illusion
of scarcity—I mean those of us who have a choice—is
more than mere politics or economics. At bottom, it has to
do with our sense of identity. Most of us gain our sense of
self not from what we share with others, but from the ways
we are different from them. I define myself not in terms of
what you and I have in common, but by what I have that
you don't and what you have that I don't. I define myself
in relation to scarcities which we possess unequally.

Somewhere, deep within us, we fear commonality. We
want to be unique, different, individual. We hardly notice
those things in which we are similar, but we are sharply
aware of those ways in which we are different. We know
quickly the imbalances that exist between us—in wealth,
and personality, and clothing, and education. When we
meet, we instantly ask for evidence of our differences:
What is your job? Where did you go to school? And
behind it all is the weighing and the measuring, the assessment of who has more and who has less, the search for our
distinctions.

Why the need to feel different, to distinguish ourselves
from the mass? Perhaps because sameness seems like a
kind of death to us, a sort of drowning in the sea of
humanity. We are always struggling to keep our heads
above water, to "stand out," as if this would save our
lives. In fact, as any swimmer knows, the trick is to relax
into the water and rely upon its ability to support a body
that does not fight it. But we seem so to fear the death of
our distinctions that we fight to rise above the very
medium which would hold us up.

In theological terms, I am speaking here of the problem
of idolatry. For by gaining identity from the possession of

scarce goods, we are establishing those goods as gods in our lives. We give these gods the power to make us happy or miserable; the power to discriminate among people, separating the worthy from the unworthy, the better from the worse. By attaching our identity to that which only a few can have, we ignore the intrinsic preciousness of all human life. Worse still, we help maintain a social structure which gives some people an exaggerated sense of worth while discouraging others from ever feeling worthy at all.

## THE GOSPEL OF ABUNDANCE

So abundance and scarcity turn out to be not conditions external to our lives, but deeply spiritual matters. When we cling to the world's resources—whether those be material or not—we create political and economic scarcity. But that scarcity is a reflection of our inner condition, a condition in which we believe that meaning will come through clinging. Of course, the more we cling, the more meaning recedes; no matter how many scarce things we have, we always want more.

In contrast to this grasping at life is the emphasis on "letting go" so central to all great spiritual traditions. In Zen, the path is one of constantly emptying the vessel, of not letting the mind hold on to any idea or experience or desire or image. In all the Eastern meditative disciplines so popular today the key is to relax and release the will, to let go of all false securities, so that one may be occupied by the power of reality and truth.

But we need not turn to non-Christian traditions to find this path. For throughout the Bible, and at the core of the Gospel, we find constant emphasis on trusting God's abundance and living beyond our fears of scarcity. "See how the lilies grow," says Jesus, "they do not toil, or spin, and yet I tell you that even Solomon in all his glory was not arrayed like one of these. If God, then, so clothes the grasses which live today in the fields and will feed the ovens tomorrow, will he not be much more ready to clothe you, men of little faith? You should not be asking, then, what you are to eat or drink, and living in suspense of mind; it is for the heathen world to busy itself over such things; your Father knows well that you need them. No, make it your first care to find the kingdom of God, and all these things shall be yours without the asking'' (Lk 12:26-31).

At the heart of letting go is faith and trust. If we do not trust that "your Father knows well that you need them," we will grasp at the necessities and even at the luxuries; if we have no faith that God will provide, we can only hoard against an uncertain tomorrow. But why trust? What is the warrant for faith? The world seems full of examples which make trust the faith of fools. Is it not prudent to be suspicious, to take nothing for granted, to store up against a hostile future? So long as even a few operate this way, they create a climate in which trust seems self-defeating.

Perhaps even this situation, with its self-fulfilling anxieties and its illusions of security, is part of God's providence. For it is precisely by thinking that we can buy our security, and then by experiencing the loss of all that "moth and rust doth corrupt," that most of us are given a chance at conversion. Perhaps most of us can learn the paradox of scarcity and abundance only by being broken in our efforts to put money or status or material well-being in the place of God.

And what is this paradox? Simply that "he who seeks his life shall lose it, but he who loses his life for my sake shall find it." True abundance comes not to those set on securing wealth, but to those who are willing to share a life of apparent scarcity. Those who seek well-being, who grasp for more than their share, will find life pinched and fearful. They will reap only the anxiety of needing more, and the fear that someday it will all be taken away. But those who live in ways which allow others to live as well, those who reach out in service to their brothers and sisters with confidence that God will meet their needs, they will find a life of plenty which transcends the economics of scarcity.

Surely, this is a conversion. For in this spiritual wisdom, the world's logic is turned exactly upside down. Grasping brings less, and letting go brings more. What God wants from our fear of scarcity is not an obsessive capitalism, but the painful spiritual lesson that we cannot buy the security and identity we seek. Those will come to us only as we let go and live in the grace of God, and in solidarity with those for whom scarcity is no illusion but a matter of life and death.

As we move toward such solidarity we will learn that people who know material scarcity often know spiritual abundance far better than we. Those who have always had to find a trust beyond the world of scarce resources can be our guides in the spiritual journey. They are the ones to whom Jesus was closest; they are the last whom the Gospel makes first. In their lives the Gospel paradox of scarcity and abundance is made manifest: "He who seeks his life shall lose it, but he who loses his life for my sake shall find it." The last *shall* be first among us.

## THE WAY OF EDUCATION

What are the ways to move beyond the self-fulfilling prophecy of scarcity into a world of shared abundance? How can we and the institutions around us respond? I want to speak of three ways—the way of education, the way of community, and the way of prayer.

It is ironic that education, which could be a mass producer of abundance, is so deeply implicated in the system of scarcity. For the primary function of the school in our society is to hand out credentials which entitle some to more, and others to less, of the good things in life. Not only does the school allocate the scarce resources of the larger society (such as access to jobs and wealth and power) but the educational process itself has become a competition over scarce goods. For instance, it should be possible to bring everyone in a class of fifty to a level of excellence in a subject; it should be possible to hand out fifty "A's" at the end of a term. Not only should this be possible, but it should be a measure of good teaching to be able to do it! And yet in few schools is this the case. Instead, we have the absurdity of "grading on the curve," or something like it, a system in which only a small percentage of the grades can be "A," a somewhat larger percentage "B," the largest group "C," then dwindling down again to a few mandatory grades of "F." Nowhere is there a better illustration of taking abundance and making scarcity. What could be more abundant than the potential for understanding? What could be more ludicrous—and tragic—than a system which forces people to compete over this plentiful commodity as if there were not enough to go around?

The schools provide one of the clearest illustrations of our belief that even in the midst of abundance, competition is the best way to determine who gets what. Why, for example, are virtually all academic exercises designed to be done by individuals in isolation rather than by groups working together? Why, indeed, when one of the most pressing needs of modern society is to train people in cooperative work? The reason is a deep-seated belief that only through competition will the goal be reached quickly and efficiently. It matters not that the goal of education is truth—whose attainment surely requires more than individual effort! So deeply do we believe in competition that we will use it as a means to any end.

Behind the belief in competition is, again, the assumption of scarcity. In the case of our schools we aim to turn out people competent at certain jobs—for example, the skilled surgeon. We are quite certain that unless we reward only a few students for exceptional effort, and punish those who fall short by comparison, our surgeons will be hacks. We are quite certain, that is, that competence is in short supply and that only a few can attain it. But what we produce, of course, is medical schools in which cheating and cutthroat tactics are rampant, and a medical industry which not only exploits the consumer but falls far short of the quality one might expect in a country as affluent as ours. The prophecy of scarcity fulfills itself in our short supply of doctors and the high price of medical services. Where we might educate doctors in ways that create abundant public health, we instead train them in habits of competition and scarcity that diminish us all.

The true calling of the educator is to be a midwife of abundance. The classical definition of education—to "draw out"—gives us our image, for the abundance of which we speak is found within each person and waits to be "drawn out." Again, our assumptions become critical, in this case our assumptions about human nature. I assume that each person contains all the potentials which education wishes to cultivate: insight, capacity for observation and analysis, ability to appreciate, creative energy. The trick is to create enough trust and self-affirmation to let that potential loose. But conventional education seems to assume either that people don't have these potentials (and so must be supplied from without), or that human nature perversely refuses to fulfill what potential it has (and so must be coerced into doing so). We know, of course, that our assumptions about the student greatly influence what the student becomes. Studies have shown that students who are assumed to be stupid become stupid, while those assumed to be bright become bright. Which shall we choose: scarcity or abundance?

There is one fact about our schools which makes the discovery of human abundance especially difficult—I mean the tendency to be interested in cultivating only one of the human gifts, that of cognitive rationality. Our schools tend to rank people along this one dimension, thus creating the air of competition and scarcity so injurious to real learning. The alternative is for schools to recognize and cultivate the diverse ways in which people learn and know, the variety of human gifts. Some people know best with their logical minds, others with their intuition, others with their hands. Some people experience life in signs and symbols, others are more gifted at perceiving color and texture and form. Some learn through contemplation while others learn largely through action and engagement. Why cannot our schools be places where this great abundance of gifts is nurtured and celebrated and used?

The answer begins with the practices of a single teacher, a teacher who is willing to turn from the safe and structured path of competition over scarce resources and walk the less-charted ways toward abundance. Doing so involves an act of trust that abundance can be found, and thus entails risk. The risk begins with the fact that conventional teaching puts the teacher in command, doling out scarce information which only he or she controls. In teaching for abundance, the teacher loses some control by sharing power with the students; at times, the class may be teaching the teacher. Under these circumstances some teachers have difficulty maintaining their sense of worth, having become accustomed to gaining their identity from knowing something that the students don't!

Another risk lies in the fact that teaching for abundance may meet with resistance from students. Teachers who have tried find this problem especially painful, since they changed their way of teaching "for the students' sake." But conventional education, though it subjugates the student, also puts him or her in a comfortable and protected position. By convention, the student need never expose what he or she knows or feels, but only passively absorb what the teacher hands out. In teaching for abundance the student must come forth, must be vulnerable, and must respond to others. And that poses a threat which students sometimes resent and resist.

There is risk too in the reactions of colleagues toward those who try to teach for abundance. We are so deeply conditioned to think of education as a scramble for that which is in scarce supply and of competition as the only path, that the turn toward abundance arouses deep suspicions and distrust. Teachers who abandon the "discipline" of pouring "content" into "empty minds" are suspected of everything from sloth to incompetence. Methods of teaching which make students teachers and teachers students are often ridiculed as "mere rap sessions." And indeed these efforts can be less than precise, for we have little experience with them and they move against powerful currents of tradition. But we must work toward a group discipline which allows the human abundance to come forth.

In all of this we are reminded that education is an essentially religious enterprise. It deals with the deepest questions of life; it puts us at risk and thus requires trust; and it can evoke the deepest resources of individual and group. The spiritual journey is a journey toward an abundance which responds to our deepest needs. Education is a religious enterprise to the extent that it rejects the assumption that knowledge and the rewards of knowledge are scarce, and proceeds in confidence that truth is ample and available to all.

## THE WAY OF COMMUNITY

Another way toward abundance is the way of community. In fact, much of what I have said about education assumes that it must become more communal and less individualistic and competitive. But community itself deserves separate consideration, for it is a potential in many aspects of our lives—home and neighborhood and workplace, as well as school. And community, like education, turns out to be a religious matter at bottom.

Community, from one point of view, is simply a survival need for the years ahead; I mean community as a means of more widely sharing goods and services than our privatized lives will permit. Why should each family on the block have a separate laundry room when one good industrial unit could serve 20 families without strain? In some cities, food cooperatives have become popular for the same reason: Why should families go separately to the store and pay high prices when by banding together and purchasing food in bulk they can reduce the cost of eating? So community is partly a way of squeezing abundance out of dwindling resources by sharing them more fully.

But community seems impossible on practical grounds alone. Our egotism is too powerful, our individualism too deep-rooted, to maintain mere marriages of convenience. For community to endure, it must be drawn together at a deeper level, a level we can only call religious. When we are called together by a shared sense of God's abundant love, then our sometimes scarce love for one another will not tear us apart. The bond is especially powerful when what calls a community into being is the desire to share God's love with those who are least among us—with the hungry and the ill-clothed and those who have no homes. So community is an expression of abundance—the overflow of God's love among us. And community is a creator of abundance too—an abundance which comes when we pool our scarcities and find that the whole is greater than the sum of its parts. In community we have an opportunity to learn that love and trust and respect grow as you give them away; and in community we have the chance to learn that every person is worthy of such regard.

Perhaps the key feature of a community in which this happens is a fully shared round of daily life, rather than a sharply specialized division of labor. For a community to function, a large number of needs must be met. There is food to be prepared and dishes to be washed; there are crises to be weathered and decisions to be made; there is money to be gathered and money to be spent; there is study and worship and simply caring for one another. A community is a place where each person has some share in all of these things. And as a community comes together to pool its wisdom and ignorance in each of these areas, one soon learns about the abundance and variety of human gifts. One learns that the person who is so helpful in a crisis is not a leader in daily routine. One sees that the person who cannot seem to make a decision is a powerful guide in worship. One learns that gifts vary, and that each person has some but not others. One learns that the gifts we need to go ahead are present within the group—and that the group need only set the stage to allow them to come forth.

So in a good community, the needs of life are not always met by imports from the outside, but they are evoked—and sometimes "squeezed out"—from the abundance of the community itself. A strong community will not have a resident psychoanalyst to deal with the life crises of its members. Instead, the members will be thrown back upon their own resources to see how they can love one another. It is remarkable how much exists within us which we never discover until conditions demand it. A good community is one in which those conditions keep recurring!

So a community consists not of specialized professionals but of generalized amateurs. It is worth recalling the root meaning of that word "amateur"—it means "lover" or "to love." Love is finally the source of all abundance in life, and it is only when love flows from us that the abundance becomes clear. The key to curing is caring, and it seems more and more obvious that the diseases of our time will be cured not by mere professionals who keep their services scarce, but by an abundance of amateurs who care.

In these reflections on community we have some clues to a major question of our time—how to turn our large, impersonal institutions in a more communal direction. Each of the marks of community I have noted is exactly the converse of the marks of an institution. Where a community shares a full round of functions, an institution is built around one or two. Where members of a community share in all the work, an institution insists on a sharp division of labor. Where a community cultivates generalized amateurs, an institution breeds specialized professionals.

An institution can become more communal by opening itself to a wider range of human functions and needs, and by trusting its members to provide them for one another. A college, for example, constantly undercuts the possibility of community by providing specialists to perform all the support services—preparation of food, hauling of garbage, care of grounds, cleaning of buildings. If any portion of these activities were given over to the staff and students, not only would the college save money, but it would also move closer to community! Moreover, it would begin to discover the abundance of gifts that exist within it, and would learn that we depend as much on those who fix pipes as on those who pipe theories.

Obviously, it would take no less than the movement of the Holy Spirit to persuade faculties and student bodies to share in these chores! But that is said less in jest than as a

reminder that community depends on people feel
movement of the Spirit in their lives. And in our time, the
Spirit seems to be afoot. There is a great hunger for community across the land; a great need to live beyond anxiety
about scarcity and into a shared abundance. Education is a
way of helping people focus this need, and community is
the social form such education will take.


## THE WAY OF PRAYER

But underlying all must be the foundation of the
spiritual life—prayer. I do not mean "saying prayers,"
which often means little more than special pleading that
God grant me some seemingly scarce resource before my
neighbor gets it. No, I mean by prayer a life that returns
constantly to that silent, solitary place within, where God
is met and where the abundance of life becomes manifest.

The active life has a way of making us feel dependent on
things. We need a vote here, a meal there, some money or
some transportation or some support. In the rapid pace of
doing business daily with the world, we get seduced into
feeling dependent on the world's resources, and we get
roped into playing by the world's rules. These are the rules
of scarcity: They tell us that what we need to survive and
succeed is in short supply, and we had better hustle faster
than the next person lest we lose the game.

A life of prayer is one in which we know the need to
return constantly to a place removed, a place where the
claims of the world can fall away and be seen for the illusions they are. This is the heart of prayer—the journey
from illusion to truth. And of all the illusions we must con-
tend with, the illusion of scarcity is one of the most important. As we settle into a deep listening for God's word,
how ludicrous seem the grasping ways of daily life! In that
silence and solitude with God, how clear it seems that "let-

ting go" is the only thing to do, for we cannot hang on anyway! In prayer, the world's version of abundance is clearly seen as a snare and a delusion, while God's promise of abundance is perceived not as future possibility but as reality, now.

Perhaps this is the most amazing destination of the way of prayer, this sense that the abundance we need is all around us and within us at the present time. It is not something we have to wait for, not a carrot dangled by a mule-driver God who wants to encourage good behavior. Nor is it a cruel hoax perpetrated by a God who wants to punish us for our sins. Abundance is available to us now, if only we will turn and look toward it, if only we will live in ways that make it manifest.

# 6

## The Conversion of Knowledge

The apostle Paul was surely a great teacher. His teaching of a God-become-human was radical. His listeners were often hostile. And yet even now his teaching lays claim on our lives. History has not dismissed it and neither can we.

Every Christian is called to be a teacher in some way. That call takes some of us into the classrooms of schools and universities. Others teach in the family, or in the community or in places of work. If it is true, as we believe, that "in Christ all things are made new," then we must try to understand how our relation to Christ will convert our teaching and learning.

The second chapter of Paul's first letter to the church at Corinth turns out to be a tract on teaching and learning, as powerful today as when it was written. Paul describes his own teaching, its sources and style, in ways which recall Whitehead's statement that all true education is religious education. Paul talks about the inner quality a student must possess if he or she is to learn deeply and well, and we are reminded why we sometimes have trouble taking in the truth. And Paul's contrast between Spirit-filled teaching and the sophistic wisdom of his day can easily be applied to the rationalism which dominates the academic culture in our day.

The chapter contains a vision of education whose impact is strengthened by the fact that it is 2000 years old. A vision still vibrant after so many passing years is surely grounded in something of substance. Whether we teach in the classroom or out, we can learn from Paul. He deals with the timeless questions of where truth comes from and how it touches us, questions which must be in the hearts of all who know themselves called by God to teach and learn.

I

As for me, brothers, when I came to you, it was not with any show of oratory or philosophy, but simply to tell you what God had guaranteed (1 Cor 2:1).

Originally the word "professor" meant someone who made a profession, who professed a faith. To be a professor was to proclaim confidence in a power beyond all human devising, a firm ground on which people could stand. Today, the function of the professor has been nearly reversed. Now the professor is one who qualifies claims with caution, who advances only tentative truth, who accustoms students to ambiguity, whose firmest ground is the slippery theory of relativism. The most common experience of college students is to have the ground taken out from under their feet, not to be shown a place to stand. The professor today is not one who can tell you "what God had guaranteed"!

Perhaps this is why the "oratory and philosophy" of which Paul speaks are so prominent among the devices of contemporary teachers. (One is reminded of the lecturer whose notes contained this marginal comment: "Point weak here—speak louder"!) When relativity reigns, how else does one convince except by techniques of persuasion and even power? The professor who has nothing to profess will soon find him- or herself engaged in something other than the transmission of truth. For in a world of relativism there is no truth to be found. Nothing is guaranteed.

Of course, Paul would understand the importance of having the ground taken from beneath one's feet. His experience on the road to Damascus was at least as shattering as the freshman's first exposure to philosophy! But the

Damascus shake-up came not from sophistry but from the living Spirit by whom Paul was seized and addressed. Surely Paul would argue that authentic education involves the destruction of myths and the disillusion of false beliefs, for Paul would have remained Saul if he had not gone through that process.

But the one who is shaken must also hear a promise, a promise that the Spirit will enter into lives which are broken open. Great teachers will not only shatter our illusions. They will also be living witnesses to the faith that there is a place to stand when the ground gives way beneath one's feet.

## II

During my stay with you, the only knowledge I claimed to have was about Jesus, and only about him as the crucified Christ (1 Cor 2:2).

How our teaching would be transformed if we spoke only what we really knew! We might speak less, but our speaking would have new power. The listener would know that our words came from experience; that they were grounded in something that had been verified in our lives. For this is how Paul knew Christ: as a living presence in his life, a power that had grasped him and turned his life around. And this was the power of Paul's teaching, that his words reflected something that had happened, that his words pointed beyond themselves.

It is well understood in the "hardest" sciences that words and concepts must be anchored in experience, or in experiments (which, after all, are only a controlled form of experience). Perhaps it is mainly in "softer" social science and in the humanities that language has come unglued from life, leaving teachers free to build worlds that are merely academic and leaving students lost in a world that they cannot recognize as their own. Worse still, for a sizeable number of students, education becomes a substitute for experience: Because they have talked about love they think they know how to love; because they have talked about justice they think they have done justice. When our teaching and learning get divorced from experiential knowledge, we foster the great illusion that to have thought about a thing is to have lived it!

I know a teacher who has two rules in her classroom: One, only speak when you feel you must speak; two, only speak that which you truly know, or to ask what you truly want to know. In her classroom there are long periods of silence sometimes, pauses which would intimidate the typical teacher and student. But here, the silence is a kind of waiting, in expectation and hope that the kind of truth that came to Paul can also come to us. And when the silence is broken we can have some confidence that it is worthwhile to listen with care.


### III

Far from relying on any power of my own, I came among you in great "fear and trembling," and in my speeches and the sermons that I gave, there were none of the arguments that belong to philosophy; only a demonstration of the power of the Spirit. And I did this so that your faith should not depend on human philosophy but on the power of God (1 Cor 2:3-5).

Paul understands that as a teacher he is, at best, the channel for a teaching which comes from beyond him, which is larger than he, which he, left to his own devices, could not convey. He also understands that it is possible for the human personality to get in the way of great teaching, to so impress (or depress!) the listener with human qualities of style or technique that nothing of the Spirit comes through.

And so Paul knows that his own brokenness, his own "fear and trembling," can contribute to the power of his teaching. For the listener then has living testimony to the fact that God works in and through human limitation and frailty. Here is the real guarantee that the Spirit comes into lives which are broken open: not the words of the teacher, but the living fact that a broken teacher can serve as the channel of a healing communication! We are reminded of another passage from Paul: "We have this treasure in earthen vessels, to show that the transcendent power belongs to God and not to us."

Paul's comments should offer no comfort to the teacher whose "brokenness" is merely inadequacy, lack of preparation or the tendency to ad lib lessons. Sloppiness and lack of care is not what Paul means when he says he relies on no power of his own! For he tells us that he came to the teaching "in great 'fear and trembling,' " obviously feeling the weight of his calling, obviously taking it with ultimate seriousness. But paradoxically, to take teaching with ultimate seriousness is to understand that it is truth who teaches, not you; it is to get one's self out of the way. This can happen only as the teacher can profess a living truth, only as the teacher is able to pray that "God's will, not mine, be done."

## IV

But still we have a wisdom to offer those who have reached maturity: not a philosophy of our age, it is true, still less of the masters of our age, which are coming to their end (1 Cor 2:6).

Those of us who teach in schools may be shocked by the notion that Paul's teaching is for "those who have reached maturity," for we are accustomed to think of our teaching as the process by which students grow mature. But is that so? How often have we been frustrated in our efforts to teach simply because our students did not yet know enough to be teachable? There is more to life than education, and some of this "more" must happen before education can take hold. Paul Goodman once said that college is a place where people should go *after* they have learned something, so they can have a chance to think about it! College classrooms are always more alive when they contain people who have been out of school long enough to know that school is not the whole thing.

For Paul, maturity is not a matter of having "the answers." Indeed, that posture toward life is a kind of death, for it closes one off to revelation. Instead, Paul links maturity with the recognition that the "philosophy of our age," and the "masters of our age," are "coming to their end." The wise person would seem to be one who recognizes the inadequacy of conventional wisdom, the hollowness of popular conceptions of truth. The beginning of wisdom, for Paul, is not answering but questioning.

There is a clue for teaching here, because teachers so often fall into the trap of giving the answer without waiting for the question. The root meaning of the word "education" is "to draw out"—not to fill up the student with information, but to draw out something that the student already holds within. Giving answers very seldom draws people out, but questions do. Under careful and sympathetic questioning we often realize that we already know the answer to our problem, or get clues as to where that answer can be found.

The wise person, for Paul, is not content merely to be a skeptic, a cynic, a nay-sayer, as appropriate as those attitudes may be in the face of conventional wisdom. But more, the wise person has a readiness for new truth, an openness to the Spirit which responds to the questions of our hearts beyond all socially approved versions of truth.

V

It is a wisdom that none of the masters of our age have ever known, or else they would not have crucified the Lord of Glory. . . (1 Cor 2:8).

Education in our society has become a road to mastery and power. We hold education in such high regard largely because we see it as a route to higher position, greater wealth, increased status. Through education we hope to gain mastery over our own lives at the very least, and even more over other people and events. We say that "knowledge is power," and thus reveal the link we have forged between teaching and learning, on the one hand, and controlling things on the other.

Of course, it is an illusion to believe that we control life; more than that, it is idolatry. For the power of life, though in us, is beyond us. It is a power which we can never possess for ourselves but can only set our lives with or against. In Paul's time, those who had seized power and wished to maintain control were those who crucified the Lord of Glory. For God's light will always reveal the self-serving of those who take power for themselves, and they will always try to snuff out the light.

And here is another way in which education and those who educate can be complicit in the continuing crucifixion. Our educational system is blighted by the fact that society uses it to sort people into categories of "winners" and "losers," of rich and poor. For is there any question that our system of schooling, with the defeat it inflicts on some and the pride it instills in others, is deeply involved in the plight of whose who are poor and hungry and naked and imprisoned? We are told that whatever we do for the least of these, our brethren, we do for Christ. By the same token, an educational system which makes the poor even poorer is a system which crucifies Christ again.

For Paul, the right teaching was reverence, not power. Reverence means knowing that God is the only source of true power; the power that builds and heals rather than injures and destroys. And reverence means respect for all life, knowing that all men and women are gifted by God, and all are loved.

VI

. . . we teach what scripture calls: "the things that no eye has seen and no ear has heard, things beyond the mind of man, all that God has prepared for those who love him" (1 Cor 2:9).

So much of our teaching and learning deals only with those things which eye can see and ear can hear. We educate for life on the surface, not life in the depths. Most of us, when we leave the shallows of school and enter the depths of life, have to unlearn much of what we have been taught in school and learn for the first time what is good and true and beautiful. Some cannot relearn quickly enough, and simply flounder or drown in waters which their education never charted.

Again, in the hardest of the hard sciences it is well-known that truth lies beyond the world of appearances, the world available to the senses. What the scientist finally deals with are not observations, but concepts or constructs. These are probes into the mystery of matter, a mystery which can be penetrated only by theory, and then only in part; it is a mystery not given to eye and ear to understand. Rare indeed is the scientist without reverence, who would not agree with Paul that much there is which lies "beyond the mind of man."

But Paul goes further yet when he says he teaches a truth which is available only to those who love God. What an extraordinary claim—that knowledge comes only through love! In modern parlance, knowing and loving have little to do with one another; knowing is a function of the rational mind, and loving is an affair of the irrational heart. But in the biblical world, the verb "to know" was used to indicate intimacy. People of the Book understood that deep knowledge comes only from the interpenetration of the knower and the known; that truth, like a person, will let itself be known only as the knower approaches it with love.

Indeed, this is one way of looking at the Christian claim that truth is personal. Great teaching invites people into a personal relationship, the relationship of the lover to the beloved. Only so can we truly know. And far from being ancient myth, this approach to knowing the world is consistent with the most contemporary philosophies of knowledge. For we now understand that you cannot separate the observer and the observed. We know that much depends on the observer's location and movement and attitude; we know that the observer inevitably has an impact on the observed; we know that knowledge comes from relationship.

### VII

These are the very things that God has revealed to us through the Spirit, for the Spirit reaches the depths of everything, even the depths of God. After all, the depths of a man can only be known by his own spirit, not by any other man, and in the same way the depths of God can only be known by the Spirit of God (1 Cor 2:10-11).

For Paul knowledge comes when spirit speaks to spirit. If we wish to know something in depth, only such a dialogue of spirits will do. We must learn to look and listen beneath the surface, beyond appearance, where the spirit of a thing may be known. We must wait for that spirit to reveal itself, and not try to force our way in. And we must bring our own spirit along, for only spirit can understand things of the spirit.

We seem so afraid of deep knowing. Our culture keeps us on the surface of things, regarding appearances as real, and regarding "spirit" as a primitive delusion. Are we afraid because we want our knowing to be a kind of "spectator sport," something in which we do not need to get involved but can merely sit and observe? In our time "objectivity" is the most desirable characteristic of knowledge. That means that I stand over here, and the objects of my knowledge stand over there; we keep our distance so that my knowledge of the thing will remain "pure," uncontaminated by personal contact.

Behind this insistence on objectivity perhaps there is the fear that knowing by relationship means taking the risk of being known and being changed. And so it does! For when knowledge comes through spirit speaking to spirit, then our spirit is searched out, and our lives may well be changed. The kind of knowledge Paul speaks of here is no passive act, no spectator sport. Instead it is a dialogue with truth in which we come to know truth and truth comes to know us. In such knowing there is the power to alter lives.

Paul puts all this beautifully toward the end of this letter to the Corinthians. Speaking of the knowledge that will come when we see God face to face, he says: "The knowledge that I have now is imperfect; but then I shall know as fully as I am known" (13:12). Philosophers have always assumed that we can know the nature of reality because both reality and our minds have the structure of rationality, and reason can know reason. For Paul, we can know what is true because truth is a person and we are persons. Just as we can love only because we are loved, so we can know only because we are known. God's Spirit reaches out to us constantly, in love and in truth, wanting to teach us, wanting us to learn. This is the assurance on which Paul's teaching rests.

## VIII

Now instead of the spirit of the world, we have received the Spirit that comes from God, to teach us to understand the gifts that he has given us (1 Cor 2:12).

If only we could understand life as gift, that would be conversion enough. And how that understanding would transform our teaching and learning. As it is, we regard the world, the objects of knowledge, as things to be seized and possessed. We speak about "pursuing truth" as if it were a quarry to be chased down. We seek to know things so that we can master them, own them, change them, control them. And so it is that with our knowledge we often brutalize the world—as the ecologists have shown in our relations to nature. When we treat the world not as a gift but as plunder, we destroy the gift we have been given, a gift which will sustain us if we receive it in gratitude and humility.

When we fail to receive truth as gift, but pursue it and wrestle it down instead, surely the quality of our knowledge suffers. For if truth is personal, then truth, like a person, will not reveal itself as fully to one who tries to pry it open as to one who waits and listens with attention and respect. The kind of truth that matters in life does not make itself known to those who shout for it to come out, then batter down the door. The truth that matters must trust us before we can have a relationship with it.

Perhaps our problem in receiving truth as a gift is that every gift makes us dependent on the giver, especially the gift of life. When we accept such a large gift we feel a debt, an obligation, which goes against the grain of our independence and autonomy. Indeed, the very reason we wish to learn, the basis on which we sell education in our society, is that knowledge increases our ability to go it alone, and lessens the likelihood that we will be dependent on anyone. Modern education is training for autonomy, and in that context it is almost impossible to admit that knowledge itself is a gift!

But the fact is that we are dependent, and authentic knowledge produces the humility and gratitude which our dependence implies. Far from the pride and false sense of power which our schooling produces, true education teaches us that all we have is gift, and that gifts are to be enjoyed and shared, not used for dominion over others.

### XI

Therefore we teach, not in the way in which philosophy is taught, but in the way the Spirit teaches us: we teach spiritual things spiritually (1 Cor 2:13).

Paul says that the relation of teacher to learner should be like the relation of the Spirit to men and women. To teach we must understand the ways in which the Spirit teaches us.

One way is the way of freedom. The word of God is spoken and we can hear it or not. If we hear the word we can follow it or not. The response is ours, and it is free—but no matter how we respond, the word is continually spoken, a word of freedom spoken in freedom. That is, the Spirit does not coerce us into listening or following, and teachers ought not coerce their students. Indeed, unless there is freedom no real learning can occur; lacking freedom we get indoctrination, not education; authentic education always lets the student make a choice.

Second, the Spirit teaches us in love. The freedom that God gives us is not a sign that God does not care; in that freedom, God does not ignore or abandon us. The Spirit wants us to use our freedom to meet and follow God's way, a way which leads to the greatest freedom of all, freedom from death. But even when we reject that way and enslave ourselves to death in life, the Spirit does not reject us. Even then God's love persists, beckoning us out of the dark places into the light. So it must be with teacher and learner. Despite the rebuffs and rejections which teachers will experience from students, the true teacher is one who wants the best for the student, in love.

Third, the Spirit teaches us in truth. God is the great unmasker of illusions, the great destroyer of icons and idols. God's love for us is so great that he does not politely permit us to harbor false images, no matter how they may seem to comfort us. God strips those falsehoods from us no matter how naked it may make us, because it is better to live naked in truth than clothed in fantasy. So it is with the true teacher who loves his or her students too much to permit untruth to go unchallenged.

## X

An unspiritual person is one who does not accept anything of the Spirit of God; he sees it all as nonsense; it is beyond his understanding because it can only be understood by means of the Spirit. A spiritual man, on the other hand, is able to judge the value of everything, and his own value i not to be judged by other men (1 Cor 2:14-15).

Here Paul focuses on the student, the learner, on his or her readiness to understand truth. Paul reminds us that teaching is not a one-way street, and that the spirit of true teaching must be matched by a spirit of receptiveness inside the learner. The same Spirit that is at work in the teacher must be at work in the student or no conversation can occur.

So, as learners we must pray for openness to that Spirit, for a receptiveness to truth which not even the most brilliant mind necessarily has. And as teachers we must not only make room for the Spirit to move within us; we must also cultivate an atmosphere which will help open students to that movement as well. We must trust that every student has the capacity to receive the Spirit, that (as the Quakers say) there is that of God in every person. And then we must work to establish a learning environment which will bring out that often hidden potential.

Such an environment will be cooperative, not competitive; in it, persons will seek for each other's strengths and build on them, rather than ferret out weaknesses to exploit. Such an environment will encourage the exposure of ignorance rather than put the premium on right answers, for only as we reveal our hesitations and doubts can the Spirit teach us. Such an environment will treat the person whole rather than a disembodied mind, for the Spirit does not speak to minds alone.

The person who achieves receptiveness to the Spirit is, as Paul says, "able to judge the value of everything." What an extraordinary definition of authentic education! What the educated person needs to know is not the appearance of a thing (easily available to our eyes and ears) but the value of a thing, its meaning in our lives, its relation to us; that which no eye has seen and no ear has heard. To be able to judge the value of everything is to be truly educated.

And the man or woman who knows the value of things is one whose own value "is not to be judged" by other persons. Of course not! For the person who is truly educated has no need to ask his or her worth in the eyes of others. Such a person will know that he or she has ultimate value in the sight of God. The same God who comes into our midst as a plumb line, showing us the value of all things, is a God who says to each of us—no matter what our condition—"you are loved." To be educated is to know this above all else.

## XI

As scripture says: "Who can know the mind of the Lord, so who can teach him?" But we are those who have the mind of Christ (1 Cor 2:16).

". . . we are those who have the mind of Christ." How arrogant the claim sounds! Yet it is not a claim made in human pride. It is made, instead, on the basis of God's incarnation in Jesus Christ, made on the basis of God's word become flesh. Before men and women knew Christ it could rightly be said, "Who can know the mind of the Lord . . .?" But if the incarnation means anything, it means that the mind of Christ is a mind that mortals can take on. For the scandal of the Christian profession is that God took on mortality in order that mortals could take on God's life.

For teachers and learners, Paul has been spelling out the meaning of the mind of Christ throughout this chapter. In teaching and learning—as in every aspect of our lives—we are invited to become members of the body of Christ. Insofar as we do, we have the mind of Christ, for the mind directs the body. And in that mind education is transformed from training in technique to a power of transformation for our knowledge, for our persons, and for our world.